Praise for *Under the Eagle's Wing*

"Long before the 9/11 terrorist attacks, Gary Hart warned that the threats to America were changing and that our national security strategies were not keeping pace. In January 2001, Gary and his former Senate colleague Warren Rudman called for an urgent new approach to national security to meet the growing threats of catastrophic terrorism. In his new book, *Under the Eagle's Wing,* Gary takes on the question that America has so far failed to answer: What should be the organizing principles for our national security strategy? To those like me who believe that our definition of national security must encompass our energy, environmental, economic, and global health challenges and that it is imperative to think anew, this book is a priority read. Gary Hart's prescriptions for America's international leadership in a changing world should also be required reading for those who hope to lead our nation in the next administration and the Congress."

—Former U.S. senator Sam Nunn

"Americans need a visionary twenty-first-century security policy to guide us through the most dangerous international security environment since the end of World War II. Gary Hart is at his best in forcing Americans to think—hard—about their security in a world of global terror and failing states. *Under the Eagle's Wing* is a provocative read as well as a compelling vision. And it is a must-read, not just for those concerned about U.S. security policy, but also for those committed to helping shape it."

—Daniel Christman, retired lieutenant general and former assistant to the chairman, Joint Chiefs of Staff

SPEAKER'S CORNER is a provocative new series designed to stimulate, educate, and foster discussion on significant public policy topics. Written by experts in a variety of fields, these brief and engaging books should be read by anyone interested in the trends and issues that shape our society.

More thought-provoking titles
in the Speaker's Corner series

Beyond Cowboy Politics
Colorado and the New West
Adam Schrager, Sam Scinta, and Shannon Hassan, editors

The Brave New World of Health Care
What Every American Needs to Know about the Impending Health Care Crisis
Richard D. Lamm

Condition Critical
A New Moral Vision for Health Care
Richard D. Lamm and Robert H. Blank

Daddy On Board
Parenting Roles for the 21st Century
Dottie Lamm

The Enduring Wilderness
Protecting Our Natural Heritage through the Wilderness Act
Doug Scott

Ethics for a Finite World
An Essay Concerning a Sustainable Future
Herschel Elliott

God and Caesar in America
An Essay on Religion and Politics
Gary Hart

No Higher Calling, No Greater Responsibility
A Prosecutor Makes His Case
John W. Suthers

One Nation Under Guns
An Essay on an American Epidemic
Arnold Grossman

On the Clean Road Again
Biodiesel and the Future of the Family Farm
Willie Nelson

Parting Shots from My Brittle Bow
Reflections on American Politics and Life
  Eugene J. McCarthy

Power of the People
America's New Electricity Choices
  Carol Sue Tombari

Social Security and the Golden Age
An Essay on the New American Demographic
  George McGovern

Stop Global Warming
The Solution Is You!
  Laurie David

TABOR and Direct Democracy
An Essay on the End of the Republic
  Bradley J. Young

Think for Yourself!
An Essay on Cutting through the Babble, the Bias, and the Hype
  Steve Hindes

Two Wands, One Nation
An Essay on Race and Community in America
  Richard D. Lamm

A Vision for 2012
Planning for Extraordinary Change
  John L. Peterson

For more information, visit our website,
  www.fulcrumbooks.com

Under
the
Eagle's
Wing

A National Security Strategy
of the United States for 2009

Under
the
Eagle's
Wing

A National Security Strategy
of the United States for 2009

Gary Hart

FOREWORD BY William Cohen

FULCRUM
GOLDEN, COLORADO

Library of Congress Cataloging-in-Publication Data
Hart, Gary.
  Under the eagle's wing : the national security strategy of the United States for 2009 / By Gary Hart.
      p. cm. -- (Speaker's corner books)
  Includes bibliographical references.
  ISBN-13: 978-1-55591-677-0 (hardcover) 1. National security--United States. I. Title.
  UA23.H366 2007
  355'.033573--dc22

                          2007041156

Printed in Canada by Friesens Corporation
0 9 8 7 6 5 4 3 2 1

Design: Jack Lenzo

Fulcrum Publishing
4690 Table Mountain Drive, Suite 100
Golden, Colorado 80403
www.fulcrumbooks.com

... provide for the common defence ... and secure the Blessings of Liberty to ourselves and our Posterity. ...
    —*Constitution of the United States of America*

Contents

Foreword

We live today in troubled and unsettled times. The hoped-for decline of significant threats to our vital interests after the end of the Cold War has, of course, failed to material-ize. Indeed, we find ourselves confronted instead once again with an ideologically driven enemy whose avowed goal also is to threaten our way of life, but which, unlike the Soviet leadership (which was more or less willing to wait for us to collapse due to the contradictions they saw in our liberal democracy), actually seeks to carry out fur-ther violent attacks on our soil.

Because we have been unable to make much of a dent in our addiction to oil, we become in a sense our enemy's financiers, as petrodollars inevitably find their way into terrorists' hands. Our addiction to twentieth-century energy policies and our refusal to develop seriously both alternative sources and means of transportation also threatens increasingly our environment: the rising annual median temperatures, the shrinking polar ice caps, and the abnormal cycle of drought we have recently witnessed bear testimony that our heavy reliance on carbon-based fuels continues to threaten this fragile planet. Our tra-ditional allies appear inclined more and more to go their own way, even as we commit resources to protect not only our way of life, but theirs as well. As we look toward the upcoming presidential campaign and a new administra-tion, it is little wonder that many Americans wonder if the United States is not as able as we once were to provide for our own security, to say nothing of the security of our friends and allies.

In this national security strategy for 2009, Senator Gary Hart has provided a characteristically cogent and well-argued blueprint for addressing the wide array of problems we face. His work is not for fans of the status quo. He calls for bold new ideas and new approaches. But it is clear that the tired nostrums and policies of the past are not working; Senator Hart, drawing on his decades-long expertise in security issues, has provided a much needed wake-up call to take action now.

A major premise of his work is that "in the twenty-first century, we will have increasing difficulty distinguishing the security of some from the security of all." From this simple yet very important observation springs a series of policy imperatives:

- The security of liberal democracies is inescapably a common endeavor.
- The United States must be "the watchman on the tower" for the global commons and must organize global security networks that can avert international catastrophes rather than have to deal with their consequences.
- The United States government, placing renewed emphasis on diplomacy and international leadership, needs to build consensus on the fact that viral pandemics, proliferation of weapons of mass destruction, global warming, and virulent conflicts spawned by ancient grievances and state failure do not recognize national boundaries, and therefore require common policies, the development of advanced political, economic, scientific, and military capabilities, and common determination to bring these to bear before events in one part of the globe spin out of control to affect the lives of all of us.

And while it is to the liberal democracies that this call is issued, Senator Hart is quick to point out that it would be foolish, indeed dangerous, not to reach out to others—to Russia, to China, and even to Iran—to encourage those governments to assume greater responsibility to work with neighbors for stability in their own regions.

Closer to home, Senator Hart offers a series of prescriptions for adapting America's military in the twenty-first century. Those familiar with his previous writings will not be surprised by his call for smaller, lighter, more lethal, and more agile ground forces and for taking greater advantage of our maritime capabilities. He calls as well for strengthening the role of the National Guard in Homeland Security and for streamlining and overhauling the Department of Homeland Security to better enable it to carry out its vital task of protecting this country. Importantly, and not to be ignored, is his injunction that the president must ensure close cooperation between the Departments of State and Defense; we know what happens when departmental rivalries and policies supplant or even substitute for concerted national effort. A new president would do well to pay close attention to this as new cabinet officers are being selected. Lastly, on pages 86–87, Senator Hart prescribes seven rules that should govern the decision to commit American military forces to combat; this discussion is extremely timely, and I hope his approach sparks a national debate. We owe our brave men and women in uniform nothing less.

I have known and admired Gary Hart for many years. His contributions to our national security over the years have been real and important. This national security strategy makes clear that he remains a thoughtful leader in the effort to make the United States safer and more secure.

—William Cohen, (R-ME) U.S. Senator 1979–1997,
Secretary of Defense 1997–2001

Introduction
A National Security Strategy for the American Republic

How does a republic make itself secure in a revolutionary age without yielding to the temptations of empire?

We Americans are in constant need of reminding ourselves that our nation was founded as a republic and, at least in principle, remains one. This reminder is necessary because the distinctive qualities of the American republic dictate what we can, and cannot, do to make ourselves secure. Our republican ideals increase our strength but also condition our conduct.

Our republican ideals include civic virtue, the sovereignty of the people, resistance to corruption, and a sense of the commonwealth. Civic virtue requires us all to participate in the search for security. The sovereignty of the people means that a president, even as commander in chief, cannot declare himself above the law and usurp our sovereignty. We must resist the corruption that puts the interests and security of the few above the interests and security of all. And our sense of the common good means that where security is concerned, we are all in this together.

Following the September 11 terrorist attacks, the president claimed extraordinary powers, including warrantless surveillance of massive numbers of Americans, in the name of national security. By its conduct of foreign policy, especially in the Middle East, the previous Bush administration undertook imperial actions incompatible with a republic.

The issue, therefore, is whether a national security

policy for the twenty-first century can preserve our republican principles and ideals and resist the temptations of empire. In the name of achieving security, republican Rome in the first century B.C. became an empire. In the throes of great fear, nations, like individuals, are tempted to do whatever it takes, to grasp at expedient measures such as surrendering their liberties and freedoms, to protect themselves.

> The issue, therefore, is whether a national security policy for the twenty-first century can preserve our republican principles and ideals and resist the temptations of empire.

Twenty-first-century Americans must not do that. We need not do that. We can and must make ourselves secure while preserving our constitutional principles. At stake is our very character as a nation.

To be relevant, a national security strategy must take into account a number of factors:

It must be rooted in America's national experience, including in its wars, and it must be consistent with our national character and our constitutional principles;

It must take into account geography and resources, as well as national vulnerabilities;

It must consider the influence of time, be capable of evolution, and be adaptable to changing circumstances;

It must understand our military cultures and values;

It must embrace statecraft, which presumes a sense of history, and must incorporate the necessity of constructing new alliances.

A national security strategy for the early twenty-first century is in part a description of how the United States, a power above all others, should behave in a twenty-first-century revolutionary world.

During the latter years of the Cold War and continuing on into the twenty-first century "war on terrorism," U.S. presidents and their advisors have outlined a national security strategy for the nation. The national security strategy produced by the administration of President George W. Bush in September 2002, a year after terrorist attacks on New York and Washington, in large part was in the mainstream of traditional security thinking. But it was exceptional in two important points: it announced the intention of that administration to engage in preemptive warfare when it deemed it appropriate to do so and it declared that the United States reserved the right to take unilateral military action, also when it deemed it appropriate.

As applied to Iraq and the Middle East, these propositions were based on at least three significant assumptions: first, democratic forms of governance and market capitalism are uniformly exportable; second, military power is the most accessible method of power exertion; and third, taken together, these propositions, combined with preemptive unilateralism, amount to a commitment to Pax Americana.

Neither of these pronouncements in and of itself is without precedent. Under international law, every nation possesses the right to act preemptively in its own security interest. What was exceptional, both in this pronouncement and its subsequent implementation in Iraq, was abandonment of the traditional international legal standard that conditions preemptive warfare on the existence of a threat that is immediate and unavoidable. In addition, history and international law assume each nation may act unilaterally to protect its security. Once again, however, the application of unilateral military action against Iraq, using "coalition forces" as a substitute for its traditional security alliances, raised the possibility that the United States could apply the same unilateral standard to Iran, Syria, North Korea, or in any one of a number of troublesome venues.

War on terrorism, preemption, and unilateralism are national security lights that have failed. Therefore, it is necessary for a new administration to outline a new approach to post–Cold War U.S. national security, an approach that takes into account the economic transformations brought on by globalization and the information revolution, the reality of failed and failing states, nonmilitary threats from pandemics and mass migration, the proliferation of weapons of mass destruction, climate alterations, and the emergence of stateless nations.

The central challenge to American diplomacy and security strategy now is to manage the globalization revolution, to take advantage of its opportunities and to reduce its risks. The dramatic integration of markets, finance, and commerce has increased the chances of improving the human condition for tens of millions even as it has weakened state sovereignty and eased the transit of villainy. Expanding markets broaden the opportunity for participation by those of good intention even as their darker corners harbor those who barter in the instruments of mass destruction.

> War on terrorism, preemption, and unilateralism· are national security lights that have failed. Therefore, it is necessary for a new administration to outline a new approach to post–Cold War U.S. national security.

The porous borders of the global marketplace allow rivers of change, ranging from new political ideas such as democracy to the threat of Western popular culture, to flood the plains and valleys of traditional societies. Old systems with established hierarchies do not surrender to dramatic change gladly. Particularly when confronted with the presence of foreign military forces, as we now know they often respond with anger and with suicidal sectarian violence.

As we have discovered to our discomfort, the most productive response to insurgent resistance is not to open the floodgates farther and line the rivers of revolution with a mighty army. This failed experiment will either further alienate us from the world that we should help lead or it will make us wiser. It is too soon to judge. At this moment, however, we are reaping the consequences of a failed strategy. These consequences have placed unnecessary strains on U.S. leadership and are resulting in the search by other powers and regional alliances for ways of balancing and restraining U.S. power that others, including traditional allies, find arrogant, hubristic, and even adolescent.

For those who see power primarily in military terms, these balancing efforts represent challenges to our leadership or even threats. Most often, however, they represent centers of economic competition and political divergence from a U.S. policy now seen by much of the world as extraordinarily self-absorbed and self-interested.

Instead, the new departure proposed by this security strategy, involving an expanded understanding of the meaning of security, has several premises. It recognizes that part of the twenty-first-century world is rapidly moving toward economic integration while other parts of the world are either stranded on the islands of tradition or, in a few cases, are threatened by political disintegration. This strategy appreciates the need

> This strategy appreciates the need to create a global commons composed of liberal democracies that will further economic integration and collective security.

to create a global commons composed of liberal democracies that will further economic integration and collective security. This approach uses the incentives of participation in economic growth and collective security to encourage the political reforms in other nations that are required to qualify for membership in the global commons. And, perhaps most importantly, this national security strategy advocates restoration of America's constitutional principles as the guideposts of our conduct in the world.

Such is the central theme of this national security strategy. This document is meant to be the framework for a larger understanding of security and how it may be achieved by the newly elected president and administration.

And, perhaps most importantly, this national security strategy advocates restoration of America's constitutional principles as the guideposts of our conduct in the world.

Part I. America's Role in the World of the Twenty-First Century

The Watchman on the Tower:
An Overview of America's International Strategy

The United States must become the watchman on the tower, warning the nations of the world of impending dangers but also foreseeing opportunities to avoid or neutralize those threats.

For almost two decades since the end of the Cold War, the United States has drifted into the twenty-first century without a comprehensive strategy concerning its place in the world. The central organizing principle of containment of communism has been replaced by a war on terrorism. This war paradigm defines America's role in the new century much too narrowly, erodes our credibility and leadership authority, and prevents us from addressing a wider range of new realities.

Throughout most of our history, the United States has sought to remain aloof from foreign entanglements. Even as factions formed for or against England and France in our formative years and those factions became de facto political parties, our most prescient leaders understood the limits of the new nation's powers and, more importantly, the corruption of the American ideal that would flow from "power politics." Thereafter until World War I, with the notable exceptions of the Spanish-American War and the border Mexican-American War, we remained an island fortress even as we grew. Against much popular reluctance, the United States emerged as a full-fledged global power by its participation in two world wars and leadership in the Cold War.

Today, America's powers are economic, political, and military. We are unrivaled in all three categories. When our behavior toward other nations conforms to the principles upon which our constitutional republic is based, we also have the leadership authority those principles provide. Principled authority is moral authority. Our founding principles both empower us and constrain us. They empower us to challenge other nations to conform to standards of human rights and democratic ideals. They constrain us from acting contrary to those same ideals. When during both the Cold War and the war on terrorism we have acted contrary to our principles, we have lost both stature and moral authority in the world community.

> When our behavior toward other nations conforms to the principles upon which our constitutional republic is based, we also have the leadership authority those principles provide.

At issue now is the appropriate conduct of a superpower and, in our case, the conduct of a superpower making claims of historically lofty ideals. More precisely, how should a superpower making noble claims use its powers? In recent years some have believed that we had not only a right but also a duty to demonstrate "strength" through the use of military force. In the case of the Taliban harboring al Qaeda in Afghanistan, that contention had virtually universal international support. In superpower conduct, however, the particular does not always provide proof for the general. As a result of the Iraq war, many nations, including friendly nations, now question the judgment of the world's great superpower on matters of great consequence.

America's founders rooted their Declaration of Independence and our Constitution in reality. They understood the conditions of the world in which they lived. But they looked beyond the immediate realities of their day to eternal truths about human aspirations, nobility, and entitlements. These truths concerning liberty, justice, and rights permeate the American character and hold us, in the eyes of the world, to account. They hold us, and we hold ourselves, to a higher standard of conduct both at home and abroad than

> When we lower our standards to conform to the less principled behavior of other nations, usually in the interest of expediency, we betray our heritage and sacrifice the authority we derive from our principles.

most, if not all, of history's great powers. When we lower our standards to conform to the less principled behavior of other nations, usually in the interest of expediency, we betray our heritage and sacrifice the authority we derive from our principles.

In the conduct of our relations with the nations of the world, our principles require that our actions be characterized by integrity, transparency, and consistency. We must be honest. Except under the most extraordinary circumstances, we must resist deception and covert conduct. And we must do what we declare we are going to do. Threats to our security prevent us from revealing every defensive action from those who would do us harm. But excuses must not be found to create a permanent state of fear that is used to justify constant deception, including of our own people, and suspension of our principles. Political leaders who cry wolf too often, especially as a method for coercing conduct, eventually lose the confidence of the American people.

The United States must align its international behavior and self-interest with the better angels of human nature and the highest aspirations of humankind. We must seek the highest, not the lowest, common denominators among the nations of the world. Wherever possible, by our actions and conduct we should seek to raise the sights of those who have not had the benefit of our constitutional heritage. In most cases what is wise and just is also what is most effective.

The United States fully subscribes to the Universal Declaration of Human Rights adopted by the United Nations in December 1948. Its first article reads "All human beings are born free and equal in dignity and rights. They are endowed with reason and conscience and should act towards one another in a spirit of brotherhood." We hold ourselves to those ideals, and we seek to hold all other nations to them as well.

As the realities we now confront in the twenty-first century are new, so our understanding of the meaning of security, both national and international, must be new and more inclusive. These realities include proliferation of weapons of mass destruction; failed and failing states; the rise of ethnic nationalism, religious fundamentalism, and tribalism; climate change and global warming; the potential for pandemics; mass south-north migrations; and the emergence of new centers of economic power.

> As the realities we now confront in the twenty-first century are new, so our understanding of the meaning of security, both national and international, must be new and more inclusive.

Our age is being revolutionized by globalization, the information revolution, erosion of national sovereignty, and the changing nature of conflict.

Further, in the world of the twenty-first century everything is closer together, the pace of change is exceptionally rapid, insecurity arises from many quarters, and unpredicted events occur much more frequently.

As global society changes, so must our concept of national security expand. Globalization and the integration of economies provide opportunities for all to rise, but they also cause economic downturns to be much more widespread. Epidemics that formerly were local or regional can now, due to mass travel, become global pandemics. Biotechnologies offer the promise of miraculous new cures but also, in the hands of evildoers, contain the threat of genocidal disaster.

These realities and revolutions require a new understanding of the nature of security. Unlike during much of the past century, twenty-first-century security will be increasingly international and will be decreasingly achieved through military means. The security of one or a few nations will require the security of most, if not all, nations. If international markets are unstable, America's participation in and economic dependence upon those markets will be unstable. The ubiquity of information diminishes any nation's ability to act surreptitiously, especially with regard to its own citizens. The failure of a state endangers the stability of its region, and the failure of a large state may endanger the stability of the world. The ability of stateless nations to attack nation-states now blurs the distinction between war and crime and threatens the security of the global commons.

> The ability of stateless nations to attack nation-states now blurs the distinction between war and crime and threatens the security of the global commons.

The framework for modern international relations is generally considered to have emerged from the multi-treaty Peace of Westphalia in 1648. After years of negotiations among the Holy Roman Empire and the house of Hapsburgs and leading European powers, the Westphalian settlement wrote the end of the Empire and introduced the nation-state concept as the basis for the political organization of Europe. This concept was premised on the bargain between nations, or peoples, and states, or governments, whereby the nation pledged its loyalty to the state in exchange for the state's guarantee of national security, a bargain requiring the state to demand a monopoly on violence.

Now the very nature of post-Westphalian nation-state sovereignty is evolving. New realities and visionary leadership will demand a more sophisticated understanding of sovereignty. Whereas in the past three centuries sovereignty was the definition of nation-state identity and authenticity, in the twenty-first century nations will retain their sovereignty by synchronizing it with the sovereignty of allies. In the realm of security, the emergence of the global commons causes the insecurity of one nation to increase the insecurity of many, if not all, nations. National security is increasingly dependent on international security and, therefore, national sovereignties and the security forces they command will increasingly be pooled to achieve collective security.

> National security is increasingly dependent on international security and, therefore, national sovereignties and the security forces they command will increasingly be pooled to achieve collective security.

Collaborative and cooperative security measures do not require sacrifice of national control and authority over our own security forces and structures. They simply require closer cooperation in training, equipping, and operating with the forces of allied nations. The North Atlantic Treaty Organization (NATO) is a forerunner of this emerging collective security regime.

The security of the global commons must be the goal of all nations of good will. The security of the United States will be increasingly inseparable from the security of other nations. Given its economic, military, and technological advantages, the role of the United States will be that of watchman on the tower, seeing farther ahead, apprehending danger, and organizing the community of nations *in advance* of immediate danger to prevent encroachment upon the security of the commons.

Nations outside the global commons, by choice or

circumstance, will increasingly find it desirable to be protected by its security umbrella and will make accommodations to liberal democracy in order to do so. The price of membership in the commons and enjoyment of its security will be the adoption of liberal democratic principles and institutions such as the rule of law, gender equality, transparent economics and electoral processes, a free press, and opposition politics. Our security strategy must be sufficiently flexible to encourage the expansion of the common security arena. Instead of setting aside our principles to accommodate oligarchies and dictatorships to obtain resources and achieve security alliances, we must make participation in the security of the commons attractive enough that they will find it necessary to adopt liberal democratic principles and ideals to obtain membership.

Grand strategy is the application of a nation's powers to the achievement of its large purposes. Our historic powers are economic, political, and military. Our unique cultural power is contained in our constitutional principles. Because our principles, properly adhered to, provide a form of moral authority, they represent a power greater than the other three powers. By applying these powers to the achievement of our large purposes—security for ourselves and our allies, the expansion of economic opportunity, and the promotion of liberal democracy—we will have formed the framework of our national grand strategy. All our powers must be wisely applied in an age of transformation. Their wise and principled application is also the most effective way for our nation to become secure.

As we carry out our role as the world's watchman and use our scientific and technological skills as well as the accumulated experience of our history in doing so, we will engender the international trust, good will, and cooperation necessary to enhance our own security and that of others. Our leadership will be characterized more by anticipation and less by reaction. And it will be seen as less self-interested and more honorable.

Guardian of the Commons:
A Twenty-First-Century International Order

In the twenty-first century, we will have increasing difficulty distinguishing the security of some from the security of all. The post-Westphalian paradigm of national security that prevailed through much of the twentieth century—national armies defending national territories—is being seriously eroded as a foundational principle by a new set of revolutionary circumstances.

The new twenty-first-century security demands that nations collaborate across cultural and ideological barriers and across national borders to achieve common goals. This new security regime will require global adaptation. Common threats will transcend political barriers and social differences. Many nations will find it increasingly necessary to set aside ancient sectarian grievances and traditional ethnic conflicts in a common search for stability and security. This century's realities, including some new threats, do not recognize national boundaries. A jihad has been declared against much of Western civilization. Viral pandemics do not acknowledge borders. The failure of states destabilizes whole regions. Weapons proliferation threatens many nations.

Traditional wars between nation-states are declining, and unconventional conflicts involving stateless nations, or non-state actors, are dramatically increasing. Therefore, the chances of the United States finding itself engaged in prolonged nation-state wars such as the two world wars are diminishing. But the chance that we and our allies will be subject to attacks by stateless nations is expanding. And, given access to weapons of mass destruction, such attacks could be catastrophic.

For the United States, our principles will not change. But many of our methods must. Where the uses and devices of terrorism are confronted, we will find it more effective to employ integrated crime-fighting and law enforcement capabilities rather than resort to conventional military forces to deter and destroy them. These capabilities— intelligence and information, penetration of cults and cells, paramilitary and special operations, and legitimate pre-emption—will increasingly take the form of multinational forces rather than the more proscribed capabilities of even the most powerful nation, the United States.

A number of nations have more skills and experience at combating abhorrent movements than we do and are more adept at handling languages and cultural traditions than we are. We will find it necessary to take advantage of these assets.

Advanced economies and stable democracies, with much to lose, will embrace the notion of the security of the commons more readily than less advantaged nations and will form the core of the secure commons. They will invite partnership and participation in ever-widening circles to nations willing to adopt democratic institutions and principles in exchange for collaborative security structures.

This is the twenty-first century's grand bargain: a protective umbrella of common security in exchange for adoption of liberal democracy.

Founding the security of the commons on the existing network of liberal democracies has a pragmatic as well as a conceptual basis. Nations sharing common values and similar political and economic institutions are able to reach consensus, and thus act, more quickly. The United Nations is a crucial organization that, six decades on, proves its worth repeatedly. But its shortcomings are endemic to its inclusive nature. Reaching consensus across cultural, political, and economic barriers among

192 nations is difficult. Reaching it quickly is impossible. Darfur is a current case in point, as Rwanda was before it. Too often nations wait for the United States to act, or not, then join us or, again too often, merely criticize.

In an increasing number of security-related instances we will not have the luxury of time. Due to rapidly evolving and unexpected challenges, a premium will be placed on deliberative but prompt action.

A new alliance of liberal democracies will supplement but not replace existing international institutions and arrangements. Placed on an extended foundation, a house is not threatened by the addition of a new wing.

An ever-expanding circle of nations will accept the notion that the security of individual nations is increasingly inseparable from the security of the global commons.

Among their shared interests are the security of energy supplies, especially international oil flows, protected trade routes, control of mass migrations, the invulnerability of strategic straits and choke points, and a common interest in reversing climate change. Likewise, all nations share an interest in preventing pandemics and in creating a web of national health services integrated in training and resources to confine rapidly spreading viruses.

The role of the United States is to organize these global security networks. The four most obvious immediate needs are, first, to create a new international security organization combining intelligence, law enforcement, and paramilitary services to disrupt and crush jihadi terrorist networks; second, to strengthen international protections against proliferation of weapons of mass destruction; third, to integrate public health services to collectively isolate dangerous pandemic viruses; and fourth, to negotiate an enforceable international treaty to reverse global warming.

More than at any time since the evolution of the nation-state in the mid-seventeenth century, substate actors are on the rise. As nation-states disintegrate and states fail, ensuing political vacuums are filled by tribes, clans, and gangs. Disintegration raises new political threats to security and stability. These include the rise of subgovernments: ancient tribes, criminal syndicates, fanatical religious factions, and ethnic nationalities. Social disintegration is always a threat to stability. It becomes even more so when its political fragments and offshoots gain access to weapons of mass destruction. This confluence of political disintegration and access to highly dangerous weapons represents global society's most immediate threat. Taken together, the combination of weapons of mass destruction, political fragmentation of nation-states, and eschatological fanaticism represents the most significant danger to the security of the global commons.

> More than at any time since the evolution of the nation-state in the mid-seventeenth century, substate actors are on the rise. As nation-states disintegrate and states fail, ensuing political vacuums are filled by tribes, clans, and gangs.

For the United States to provide genuine leadership to appreciate these new realities and to forestall them from becoming genuine threats will require us to accept the notion of collective sovereignty, not the sacrifice of sovereignty, and to think as creatively regarding new international institutions as our leaders did in the mid-twentieth-century interim between the end of World War II and the dawn of the Cold War.

From our World War II and Cold War experiences we learned the importance of alliance and common defense with like-minded nations. Both required skillful diplomacy and sophisticated appreciation for the opinions of allies for military operations, offensive and defensive, to succeed. Until it was shattered by the invasion of Iraq, common defense characterized our approach to national and international security for six decades. Stark new realities now demand that traditional alliances be restructured and new ones built.

As the realities of the twenty-first century are new, so the political and security arrangements necessary to deal with them must be new. As we created a new international order in the mid-twentieth century between the end of World War II and the beginning of the Cold War, now our existing alliances must be redesigned, and, where necessary to deal with new realities such as terrorism, new collaborative networks must be created.

The neglect of statecraft and statesmanship has prevented us from using the post–Cold War period to launch a new age of internationalism. Rather, the misadventure in Iraq represents a reversion to a pre–Atlantic Alliance era of unilateralism characterized by every man for himself and devil take the hindmost on the one hand and a mistaken attempt by the United States to become an imperial power on the other. Either way, almost two decades in which to replicate the creative era of 1945 to 1947 have been squandered.

If forces such as globalization and the information revolution are integrating much of the world, and if we now confront a host of new realities that yield only to multinational response, then the stage is set for the United States to reprise its role as global convener of a broad new alliance of the commons. Imagination is required to propose new institutional approaches to environmental protection, disease prevention, reversal of weapons proliferation, and stabilization of financial and communications systems. But, at its most creative periods, imagination has been the hallmark of the United States.

Proposals such as that for a Concert of Liberal Democracies, a potential union of sixty or so liberal democracies, deserve attention as a means of rebuilding and modernizing twentieth-century security and cooperation alliances in Europe and Asia and of laying the groundwork for new alliances to supplement them.[1] Originally proposed by the Princeton Project on National Security in September 2006 and "designed to strengthen security cooperation among the world's liberal democracies," this concert is seen as a means of achieving more-rapid integration of the security capabilities of the nations sharing common political principles and structures and of achieving consensus for common action more quickly than in forums such as the UN that are more inclusive but are also more diverse and less heterogeneous.

America's new role is to be the principal guardian of the commons and organizer of the common security. This cannot be achieved under the aegis of a theocratic foreign policy that judgmentally divides the world between the good and the evil, the saved and the damned, those who are for us and those who are against us. We possess neither the supreme wisdom nor the moral perfection to qualify us to rule by divine right.

The alternative to theocratic judgmentalism is not relativism. Nor can stability for its own sake be our ultimate benchmark, for even today close friendship with many dictatorships and oligarchies is condoned, even by theocratic thinkers, in the name of stability.

In organizing the security of the commons, neither expediency nor the presumption of divine guidance but instead the ethical guideposts and restrictions contained in our own constitutional principles must be our guide. The moral authority provided by those principles will qualify us to be the chief guardian of the commons.

Architect of Security:
A New Sense of Security for a New Century

As the United States is the world's watchman and guardian of the commons, so we must also be the principal architect of new security structures.

As distinct from the narrow understanding of security as principally a military concern, twenty-first-century security will encompass additional facets: a sense of security from the threat of proliferating weapons of mass destruction; security of communities and borders; security of livelihood and health; security of our climate and environment; and security of energy supplies. Reversal of global warming and commitment to eliminate nuclear weapons from the earth are central to this effort.

The world of the twenty-first century is presenting new and different dangers and opportunities. The opportunities must be employed to reduce the dangers. The greatest danger is in preparing for the wrong danger, as history's dustbin of failed powers can testify. Central to the security of the United States and the global commons is a clear understanding of which dangers are real and which are self-created or imaginary. The United States cannot assume responsibility for anticipating and addressing every challenge. As world leader we can assume responsibility for clearly anticipating the paths and pitfalls ahead, appealing to common security interests, and organizing nations of good purpose to collective action.

> Central to the security of the United States and the global commons is a clear understanding of which dangers are real and which are self-created or imaginary.

Our nature and character condition our conduct. The United States is a republic. As a republic we cannot also seek to become an empire and retain our republican character. As powerful as it is, the United States must not attempt to govern the world or even a major region of it. Nothing would weaken the United States more than to extend itself beyond the capacity of its own resources or to assume an imperial stance in violation of its own character. The United States must avoid the temptations and dangers of empire, even that of benign empire, above all else.

Instead, first we must appreciate our current status. In 2000, the U.S. Commission on National Security for the 21st Century issued these findings, inter alia: the United States will continue to shape the international environment through its economic, political, and military power; the advantages of science and technology will expand dramatically but remain unevenly distributed; fossil fuels will continue to be the basis of world energy supplies and uses; economic opportunities will expand, but economic disparities will increase; commerce will be increasingly global; U.S. security will be increasingly internationalized, thus raising sovereignty issues; the United States will remain the dominant military power; weapons of mass destruction will increasingly proliferate and incidents of violence will become more brutal; and alliances will be more important to U.S. security but will be more difficult to organize.[2] (The executive summary of the commission's findings and recommendations are found in Appendix II.)

Perhaps most important, certainly in retrospect, was this finding: "America will become increasingly vulnerable to hostile attack on our homeland, and our military superiority will not entirely protect us."[3] This conclusion was founded on a chilling new reality: fanatical stateless nations (fanatical jihadi organizations, most currently) are not deterred by our military supremacy and are unafraid of suicidal self-sacrifice. They represent no nation that can be conquered or capital that can be occupied.

The attacks of September 11, 2001, months after this and other warnings, proved the idea of deterrence through military strength, so central to Cold War doctrine and national defense, to be futile. Among their other symbols of national vulnerability, the attacks on America's financial and military headquarters signaled the end of the use of the rational rules of chess as a metaphor for defense theory and planning. Suicidal impulses do not yield either to diplomatic rationality or military power.

In addition, the expansion of America's economic reach and extension of its political power increase friction between us and those who resist our influence, which, in many cases, they see as threatening to their cultural traditions and values. We see the extension of our popular culture as a blessing to the less fortunate. Too often they see it as a threat to their social structures, religious beliefs, and traditional way of life. The substantial indigenous resistance our presence in Afghanistan and Iraq has created continues to make it too easy for culturally conservative and fundamentalist religious figures, especially in the Islamic world, to configure the United States as a satanic presence, a force for evil.

The search for security requires us to creatively address these and other new post–Cold War realities but also to take advantage of new opportunities to reduce these threats. Globalization, the explosion of information, declining conflict between nation-states, greater cross-border exchange and travel, rising standards of living in key societies such as China and India, and improvements in public health all represent opportunities to reduce conflicts and expand opportunity and promise.

The increasing indivisibility of security provides not only the opportunity but also the necessity of integrating security networks, systems, and capabilities. Wherever possible outside the confines of the most valued state secrets, the United States must share intelligence concerning common threats with trusted allies and encourage them to do likewise.

Shortened warning times, a shrunken globe, porous borders, and the ability of dispersed terrorist cells to coordinate multiple attacks create a much greater need to get information and intelligence quickly and, most of all, to get it right. The margin of error for intelligence failure is greatly diminished.

We will be required to conduct multinational training exercises between our special forces and those of other nations. We must operate jointly and collectively against jihadi and other terrorist groups that endanger the security of all. We will find it necessary to integrate communications systems and databases among the law enforcement and public safety agencies of liberal democratic nations.

> Shortened warning times, a shrunken globe, porous borders, and the ability of dispersed terrorist cells to coordinate multiple attacks create a much greater need to get information and intelligence quickly and, most of all, to get it right.

But integrated security systems require our natural allies and traditional friends to share the burden. Expanding intelligence networks, multiplied special forces, and enlarged paramilitary operations demand greater investment by our allies in collective security. This new world challenges our diplomacy and requires immediate repair and restoration of badly damaged traditional alliances in Europe and Asia and creation of new security alliances in East Asia and North Africa. Despite our prosperity, the United States cannot continue to finance a disproportionate share of collective security.

American taxpayers cannot finance the security of the global commons alone. But in return we must accept that greater investment by other nations will entitle them to greater voice in the management of security alliances. Too often in the recent past the United States has failed to press other democracies to expand their defenses on the grounds that we do not want military equals or rivals. As great powers in the past have proved, economic insolvency lies along the path of the quest for military supremacy.

As powerful as we are, America will multiply its power exponentially through integration of forces and through collective operations with our allies. This is the lesson of two world wars and the Cold War, and to a lesser degree Persian Gulf War I, which required a coalition of much shorter duration (and in which the United States supplied three-quarters of the manpower). Twenty-first-century security architecture will be characterized by substantially increased integration of intelligence and communications networks, joint equipping and training of special forces, collective preparation for nation stabilization and rebuilding, constabulary capabilities, and peacemaking and peacekeeping. Creation of this architecture will demand security architects with a sense of history, with imagination and vision, but also with political, diplomatic, and military leadership.

In terms of imagining twenty-first-century security, we may have recourse to the Roman fasces, a collection of sturdy rods bound together around the central symbol of an axe. Whether or not the United States assumes the role of ax, it will increasingly require the support and strength of the rods representing like-minded liberal democracies. Suggestions for a new twenty-first-century architecture, including a Global Democracy Security Organization, an expanded International Atomic Energy Agency (IAEA II), and a Zone of International Interest in the Persian Gulf, are outlined in following sections.

Part II. Organizing the Global Commons

A Force of Civilized Societies:
Law Enforcement on the Global Commons
This security strategy emphasizes the importance of managing the risks while taking advantage of the opportunities of globalization. Among the risks and challenges to be managed are threats to the security and integrity of global financial and communications systems, the security of international public health systems, codifying climate change regimes, guaranteeing the security of oil distribution systems, and the integration of emerging economic powers such as Russia, China, and India into global networks.

Many of these concerns can be addressed through expanded international alliances, networks, and treaty agreements. Some may require stronger measures. Occasions will arise where twenty-first-century security requires law enforcement carried out by something akin to the nineteenth-century American sheriff and posse.

The United States must organize a twenty-first-century international network capable of eliminating jihadi terrorism. This force will require the integration across national borders of intelligence services, special forces, and law enforcement and public safety agencies as a multinational capability to isolate and eradicate terrorist organizations. This new entity must also focus on ensuring that weapons of mass destruction do not fall into the hands of evildoers. Law enforcement and crime prevention, not warfare, will be the model employed.

The new force composed of civilized societies might, for example, be called the Global Democracy Security Organization (or NATO II). Like its predecessor, the North Atlantic Treaty Organization, designed for the age of containment of communism, the Global Democracy Security Organization should maintain a permanent command structure, headquarters, and command staff. One of its branches should be an integrated intelligence service that operates a common database on individual and group threats and a common communications system shared by member nations. A second branch should be dedicated to the excision of financial sources from terrorist organizations. Another of its branches should coordinate the activities of multinational law enforcement and public safety organizations in isolating and planning the elimination of terrorist cells once they have been identified. And a fourth branch should jointly train and exercise the special forces of the member nations to undertake the suppression of these cells.

It is important to note that the original NATO Charter, Article 12, provided for periodic review of security conditions then prevailing with the possibility of "the development of universal as well as regional arrangements under the Charter of the United Nations for the maintenance of international peace and security." (April 3, 1949) Thus, the founders of NATO left open the possibility of new security arrangements, of the sort proposed here, in light of new security threats and opportunities. (A proposed Global Democracy Security Organization charter is found in Appendix III.)

NATO has proved that compatible democracies with common security concerns can integrate military forces, cooperatively train and collectively equip them, and operate jointly in their common interest. They are doing so

even today, after a half century, in Afghanistan. These same principles of integration and cooperation can work equally well in crushing terrorist cells within its members' borders and beyond. All that is lacking is the imagination and will and the political leadership to construct this

> NATO has proved that compatible democracies with common security concerns can integrate military forces, cooperatively train and collectively equip them, and operate jointly in their common interest.

Global Democracy Security Organization out of existing national capabilities. The United States should now provide that imagination, will, and leadership. This new counterterrorism capability (whether called the Global Democracy Security Organization or something else) must be swiftly organized to provide standing capabilities to identify, isolate, and dismantle networks of those who would attack its members or disrupt international peace and stability.

Special emphasis must be placed on intelligence collection and distribution. Even among U.S. intelligence agencies, it has proved difficult to achieve openness and parity in information sharing. It will be even more difficult to expand trust among the multitude of intelligence services in progressive democracies. Knowledge is power, and power is not readily shared. But human lives, principally of innocent citizens in Madrid, Paris, London, Berlin, Washington, and New York, among many other cities, are at risk. Further, a degree of trust has been established through six decades of intelligence sharing in NATO and other formal and informal security relationships. This trust must be built upon and encouraged to flourish. Although all contingencies cannot be prepared for, to prevent specific planned attacks it is necessary to know when, where, and by whom these attacks are to occur. The very risky task of penetrating jihadi organizations is central to successful counterterrorism.

The United States Commission on National Security in 1999 outlined the kinds of forces the United States will require in a century of new and different security threats: "the type of conflict in which this country will generally engage in the first quarter of the 21st century will require sustainable military capabilities characterized by stealth, speed, range, unprecedented accuracy, lethality, strategic mobility, superior intelligence, and the overall will and ability to prevail."[4] In many respects the key qualities are "sustainable," given the exhaustion of regular and reserve U.S. forces in the prolonged Iraqi conflict, and the "will and ability to prevail," which is a political, not a military, category.

But this same description must apply to collaborative forces of various nations combined to suppress disruptive factions and to protect the security of the commons. The leadership required to develop these capabilities will test the wisdom and sophistication of U.S. diplomacy, especially our persuasive ability to forge sustainable international military and paramilitary capabilities provided by governments that have the will and ability to prevail.

A clear distinction must be made between counterinsurgency and counterterrorism operations. Though often used interchangeably and sometimes confronted simultaneously, the two are not the same. Counterinsurgency normally involves conflict between a liberating or occupying power and indigenous forces seeking its removal. Counterterrorism, under today's conditions, involves simultaneous efforts in several states and regions, some helpful and cooperative and some not, to locate, suppress, and eradicate fanatical jihadi networks involved in attacks against the homeland and interests of perceived ideological oppressors.

The confusion of insurgents with al Qaeda in Iraq continues to confound our responses even today and will continue to until our leadership has a more sophisticated appreciation for the complex, multilayered factions and disparate challenges we confront there. Calling all resistance in Iraq "al Qaeda" for U.S. political purposes is either ignorant or deceptive. A majority of Iraqis, including many not involved in the insurgency, simply want U.S. military forces out of their country.

It is crucial that the United States resist involvement in counterinsurgency warfare to the degree possible. Successful counterinsurgency campaigns have rarely been successful, and those that were, particularly in Malaysia and Singapore, managed to isolate insurgents from the larger population. Like counterinsurgency capabilities, counterterrorism forces rarely resemble traditional standing armies. They do not seek long-term occupation, and they adopt political and economic strategies that deny terrorists resources and a social sea in which to swim.

To complicate matters, not all nations employ the same standards to evaluate their security. Pakistan is a case in point. We need Pakistan's help to eradicate al Qaeda. Pakistan's government finds it necessary, or perhaps merely convenient for its own political purposes, to tolerate fundamentalist, anti-Western Islamic elements favorable to al Qaeda. It is universally accepted that al Qaeda cadres and leadership operate along the Afghan-Pakistan border and even from Pakistani territory. Thus, Pakistan is increasingly squeezed between U.S. demands that it flush al Qaeda from its midst and its indigenous fundamentalist elements' demands that it not do so.

Complex realities represented by Pakistan and much of the Islamic world illustrate the need to coalesce liberal democracies. Confronted with the financial and commercial implications of alienation from much, if not all, of the developed world, the Pakistans of the world will find themselves much more inclined to cooperate with larger security objectives.

The greatest test will be that of America's ability to persuade. Political leadership rests in the art of persuasion. The United States, once having first persuaded itself and its own citizens of the security requirements of the new century, must then persuade others, both traditional allies and emerging nations, that the security of each nation is dependent on the security of all. Where law enforcement, public safety, intelligence services, and special forces are concerned, traditional bureaucratic fiefdoms and provincial power structures will find it necessary to give way to greater collective security concerns.

> Political leadership rests in the art of persuasion.

Cooperation and coordination are small prices to pay for more-secure societies. Meshing multinational security, public safety, and intelligence agencies and services will be no easy task. But, once achieved, the results in the frustration of the plots of evildoers and the enhanced safety of millions of citizens will fully justify the effort.

On September 12, 2001, the French newspaper *Le Monde* headlined "Today we are all Americans." For the future, we must be able to say, "Today we are all citizens of the society of civilized nations, and we are more secure for it." Organizing and structuring integrated law enforcement internationally, whether along the lines of the nineteenth-century frontier or not, will be a large step toward that society.

Managing Globalization's Risks

Twenty-first-century security architecture will contain a variety of new instruments and capabilities. New realities require new capabilities: for new jobs, old tools when they are effective, new tools when they are not. Globalization has its risks, and they must be accurately understood and skillfully managed. Among the new realities that affect the stability of the global commons are rapid proliferation of weapons of mass destruction, jihadism, interruption of oil supplies, and the possibility of failed and failing states.

As with the real but more remote hazard of failing states, the greater problem of proliferation of weapons of mass destruction yields itself neither to military nor to unilateral solution. The United States is not the only nation threatened. Other nations have concerns at least equal to ours, and those concerns must coalesce into collective action. Skillful diplomacy based upon strengthened international legal networks is required to isolate rogue states and substates. Individual nations, including our own, must quarantine corporate suppliers of highly toxic and hazardous materials and equipment used in production of nuclear, biological, and chemical weapons. Even while claiming to oppose proliferation, too many advanced Western governments and new nuclear states such as Pakistan participate in the global proliferation bazaar. Proliferation is a direct product of globalization and the explosion of technology. Like terrorism itself, it will not be solved by invasion or bombing of foreign countries.

> Proliferation is a direct product of globalization and the explosion of technology. Like terrorism itself, it will not be solved by invasion or bombing of foreign countries.

We have found it productive and necessary to surround North Korea with organized opposition from China, Russia, and Japan. Likewise, in the case of Iran we are seeking the cooperation of Russia, Europe, and neighboring states in resisting its development of a nuclear weapons capability. These are instances where even the most hardened unilateralists have understood the power of multilateralism. Twenty-first-century security is a broad concept involving extramilitary capabilities and operations. Prevention of the proliferation of nuclear weapons, particularly in North Korea and Iran, is crucial and will require multinational commitment. China's role, together with that of Japan, is critical where North Korea is concerned, and Russia's role is equally critical in the case of Iran. These are not challenges facing the United States alone.

The time is overripe for a new arms control age and regime. The United States must now convene negotiations among the principal nuclear powers, including Great Britain, France, Russia, and China, with an agenda to limit the numbers and types

> The time is overripe for a new arms control age and regime.

of nuclear weapons required by each. The powers of the International Atomic Energy Agency to inspect nuclear facilities and particularly reprocessing plants must be substantially increased. And more-stringent controls must be placed on nuclear materials. Nuclear arms control and reduction were not simply a Cold War imperative. They are now more important than ever.

Both Iran and North Korea, undoubtedly as well as others to follow, sharply underscore the necessity of increasing the scope of the International Atomic Energy Agency's authority. Its resources in personnel, finances, and legal authority must be increased. Membership in the world community, or even in a new concert of democracies, must be conditioned on transparency where nuclear capacity is concerned.

The global community has both the necessity and the right to know what nations are developing weapons of mass destruction. This is the prime instance where traditional nation-state sovereignty must yield to the interests of regional and global security. The United States alone cannot police all international nuclear laboratories. Equally important is the prevention of markets for weapons of mass destruction. The head of Pakistan's nuclear program, Abdul Q. Kahn, operated his own nuclear supermarket, presumably with the knowledge, if not also approval, of his own government. Among other shoppers were the North Koreans. Al Qaeda is known to be a busy shopper in this dangerous market even today.

As with the greater threat of proliferation, the more remote, but still real, possibility of further state failure requires anticipatory preparation by advanced nations. A union of liberal democracies should create a standing intervention capability—a peacemaking force—that is trained and available to assist faltering nations and, where possible, to restructure failed states. Tribalism, ethnic nationalism, and religious fundamentalism are forces that cannot be allowed to erode international stability and devolve into a host of renegade and potentially dangerous stateless nations.

A failed state is an open invitation to the organizers of terrorism and the instigators of ethnic violence. The collapse of the former Yugoslavia and the potential collapse of Iraq, both featuring reopened old wounds and ancient animosities by ethnic nationalists and sectarian militias, represent the kind of threats to regional stability that endanger all. Resolution of the status of the various parts of the former Yugoslavia is far from settled almost two decades after its collapse. And some predict that, inevitably, Iraq will become a loose federation of three possibly warring states.

Though not a widespread occurrence, every failing state is a threat to its neighbors, and it eventually becomes a regional concern. Shortened response times require anticipation of, not reaction to, state collapse. Regional alliances must be formed to respond to such collapses before they occur. The window of time between order and chaos is narrowing. Those alliances must equip themselves to provide support networks for civil society, trained experts in maintenance of public

> The window of time between order and chaos is narrowing.

services such as public health, managers of financial, communications, and transportation systems, and constabulary and peacekeeping forces.

No single nation, including the United States, can unilaterally undertake the mounting task of repairing broken states and preventing fractured ones from collapsing. This is a task for the community of developed nations and the sixty or so liberal democracies that share common beliefs and interests. Unlike in the past century, danger in the twenty-first century comes much less from ideology and much more from the fragmentation of states. If nations can live more peacefully under the guidance of their own governments, partition and eventual reorganization of artificial nation-states, especially those arbitrarily created by colonial powers, may be required. The issue is not one of forcing rejected, second-class, or abused minorities to suffer under cruel governance. The issue is whether restructuring of fragile nation-states can be conducted in an orderly manner and whether that restructuring will protect the rights of all and leave their regions more stable.

Nation stabilization is not an idealistic notion. It is a practical necessity in a world where state failure and national fracture can threaten the balance and stability of a region, not to say also threaten the very existence of defenseless factions within the state, such as in Kosovo, Rwanda, and Darfur.

But nationhood without the semblance of an economic base is worthless. National identity at the price of starvation is not an acceptable bargain. Unsettled new states, like oppressed minorities in more settled states, are breeding grounds for radical jihadism, tribal vengeance, and fanatical causes. National sovereignty will become a more problematic and even fragile principle in this century under the pressures of globalization on the one hand and disintegrative forces such as religious fundamentalism and ethnic nationalism on the other. These disintegrative pressures will be greatest among those artificial states where disparate tribes and unrelated nationalities coexist simply because a prior colonial power dictated it. Such is the case in Iraq and is the source of much bloodshed.

No group of nations should now, in the post-colonial era, seek to act colonially and force nationhood on unlikely or incompatible groups, especially under circumstances where one faction dictates to or oppresses another. However, the family of nations cannot be passive where national disintegration threatens regional or global security. If states require assistance to prevent failure or if states require assistance to disintegrate peacefully, there must be a standing nation-structuring capability.

The United States must coordinate the creation of this new international capability, which should include multinational peacekeepers, law enforcement trainers, legal structure and health institution builders, infrastructure designers, and democracy instructors. The institutions of a stable democracy can only flourish where security is guaranteed.

To carry out an ambitious and historic transition to cooperative security, notions of collective sovereignty, whereby a concert of like-minded countries agree to pool their sovereign powers, require serious elaboration. On one level, this is not a novel idea. International treaties throughout modern history have required signatory states to limit their individual actions out of deference to the interests of other parties or to collectively agree to take positive actions in the interests of all. Arms control agreements are an instance of the former, and creation of international organizations, including the United Nations, are instances of the latter. In the twenty-first century, synchronized national sovereignties will require a further step, the integration of respective national institutions, whether law enforcement, public health, or environmental protection, to achieve desired, in some cases necessary, objectives and to carry out operations to obtain those objectives.

Even as global challenges such as arms control and failing states are addressed, special attention must be given to particularly volatile conflicts such as the Israeli-Palestinian issue. This national security strategy accepts the traditional wisdom that peace and stability throughout the Middle East is dependent on the resolution of this conflict. To believe that the U.S. invasion and occupation of other nations in the region is an alternative to this resolution is to embrace pure folly.   .

Single-minded, dedicated, fully committed diplomacy led by the United States principally but involving regional nations of good will, and not force of arms, is the only approach with any hope of success. The United States simply cannot permit, as it did for almost seven years, the unresolved Palestinian issue to continue to destabilize the entire region The United States cannot solve the problem by itself, but the issue will not be resolved without dedicated U.S. involvement. Although not altogether sufficient, vigorous and persistent U.S. leadership is necessary. By now formulas for a two-state solution are well known. Lacking are strength of purpose, political will, and statecraft.

Peacekeeping in the Middle East and elsewhere will, if anything, be in greater demand in the twenty-first century than in the twentieth. But the peace cannot be kept until the peace is made. Peacekeepers, by definition, are neither trained nor equipped to make the peace, yet UN peacekeeping forces defensively trained and equipped are criticized when they are unable to make the peace. To suppress violence in a failing state such as in the Darfur region of the Sudan or in ethnic or sectarian conflicts requires forces offensively trained and equipped. These forces must be capable of imposing peace on warring parties and factions. Then the peacekeepers may move in with diplomats and negotiators to resolve, where possible, political and religious differences.

Therefore, as an instrument of its national security strategy, the United States must undertake the task of organizing an international peacemaking force composed of multinational forces under international command. This force will not be tasked with resolving conflicts. It will be tasked with suppressing violence so that genocide and attacks on noncombatants are prevented and diplomatic resolution may be attempted without bullets buzzing overhead. The United States must undertake this task for the principle and self-interested purpose of avoiding sole responsibility as the default peacemaker in the world.

> The United States must undertake the task of organizing an international peacemaking force composed of multinational forces under international command.

Today, when crises occur, our options are either to do nothing, to intervene unilaterally, or to try to form coalitions of the willing. The fourth option of a standing international peacemaking force is required.

Nation-building and peacemaking cannot be successful unless immediately accompanied by the capability to structure civil societies and democratic institutions, including particularly legal systems, infrastructure operations, health care systems, civil administration, and educational systems. Dictator removal, as we sadly know from Iraq, does not automatically guarantee a functioning civil society, particularly in ancient cultures and in nations composed of conflicting factions. Peacemaking and nation restructuring will both be central to the security of the global commons in the current century and therefore central to a U.S. national security strategy.

Strengthening and sometimes reorganizing viable but fragile states, and the prevention of the residue of failed states devolving into stateless nations, will increasingly be central to the security of the United States. Although military power may in some cases be necessary to this cause, it will not be sufficient. Nor will unilateral U.S. action suffice. An expanding global commons will require social and political stability and avoidance of state fracture and failure.

We would not permit a family conflict in our neighborhood to devolve into gunfire and slaughter. So too in the neighborhood of nations.

A Means of Threat Reduction: Advocacy of Human Hope

Anger and resentment seldom take root in the garden of possibility and promise. Security does.

The great mass of humanity resists violence and seeks peace. Common dreams of shelter, food, medicine, employment, and care for children permeate all societies, all ethnicities, and all races. Programs of human scale and direct empowerment, replacing traditional government-to-government foreign assistance, will do much to alleviate misery and hopelessness, promote self-sufficiency and independence, and provide promise for human flourishing. The United States must organize the developed world to fashion new ways of providing water, clinics, housing, nourishment, and political empowerment at the community level to the more than 2 billion people now left out.

The twin revolutions of globalization and information technologies have increased opportunity and prosperity for most of the developed world and have provided a platform for developing nations such as

> The twin revolutions of globalization and information technologies have increased opportunity and prosperity for most of the developed world. ... But these revolutions have also widened the already considerable gap between the haves and the have-nots.

India and China to leap into the developed world. But these revolutions have also widened the already considerable gap between the haves and the have-nots and are leaving half to two-thirds of the world farther behind. Much of the less developed or underdeveloped world has little if anything to trade, whether finished products, raw materials, or services. In that world, literacy rates are so low that, except in few cases, information technologies have difficulty gaining a foothold or providing a springboard to even marginal standards of living.

The security of the commons requires that the perpetual struggle to elevate the lot of those left out must be renewed with increased vigor. Neglect is no longer an option. For neglect ensures deepening poverty, despair, and hopelessness. And hopeless people are desperate people. Desperation is the stagnant breeding pool of those with nothing to lose. Desperation is terrorism's fertile soil. Not all desperate people become terrorists, but some desperate people feel they have nothing to lose and will stop at nothing.

> Desperation is the stagnant breeding pool of those with nothing to lose. Desperation is terrorism's fertile soil.

Despair alone is not the principal cause of extremism. The tides of globalization, the confrontation by ancient and traditional cultures with the imperatives of modernity, water the roots of the age of jihad. Even more, the presence of foreign armies, now more those of the United States than of former colonial powers, ignites the fires of resistance and insurgency. Careful analysis has established that "there is little connection between suicide terrorism and Islamic fundamentalism ... Rather, what nearly all suicide terrorist attacks have in common is a specific secular and strategic goal: to compel modern democracies to withdraw military forces from territory that the terrorists consider to be their homeland."[5]

A sophisticated understanding of the complex and interwoven world of the early twenty-first century reveals layered forms of occupation. The most obvious, and the most provocative, is the presence of U.S. troops on foreign soil. These layers range down to a metaphorical "occupation" by popular culture, the sense that commercial America is being imposed on (even as it is being consumed by) traditional cultures that see it as desecration of ancient mores and beliefs. Many of these layers of supposed occupation are unavoidable in a globalized world. Nevertheless, in its public, diplomatic sector as well as in its private, commercial sector, the United States must be careful in its practices not to impose itself in ways that seem to others as a subtle form of occupation.

> In its public, diplomatic sector as well as in its private, commercial sector, the United States must be careful in its practices not to impose itself in ways that seem to others as a subtle form of occupation.

At the least, a principal element of a U.S. counterterrorism strategy must be to remove, in all cases where possible, the military presence that triggers anti-American violence. Alternative military options, and there are a number, are set out below.

In addition, however, attention must continue to be paid to economic disparities. In the developing world, especially in giant nations such as China, Russia, and India, gross national products are increasing and patterns of consumption are expanding. But these can be false measures of prosperity and security. Beneath these macroeconomic numbers deeper questions must be asked. Are rising tides lifting all boats? Are income and consumption being taxed to provide critical public services such as schools, medicine, and shelter in poorer regions? Are national efforts being made to expand the middle class and provide a social safety net for those left out? Is income being distributed nationally to rural areas as well as cities? Are the benefits produced by the private sector being made available to all, and are the services of the public sector keeping pace with the expansion of the private sector to prevent the widening of gaps between the haves and the have-nots?

Hope, the alternative to despair and the best defense against social revolution, requires that social indicators keep pace with economic indicators and that the benefits of expanding economies are fairly shared throughout societies. For emerging nations to create a class of great wealth, a small middle class, and to leave behind a disproportionately large poorer class is not a guarantor of stability or security. Wealth and economic success do not inevitably trickle down.

Some in the United States are tempted to concede defeat in the age-old struggle against endemic poverty. Others never believed in the struggle in the first place, preferring to place their hope for security in higher walls and larger weapons. This national security strategy chooses to place its confidence in the ability of advanced societies, collectively coordinated, to help the vast majority of human beings on the planet achieve at least minimal standards of living: nourishment, shelter, and medicine.

The United Nations Universal Declaration of Human Rights encompasses this goal within its definition of what it means to be a human being with rights: "Everyone has the right to a standard of living adequate for the health and well-being of himself and of his family, including food, clothing, housing and medical care and necessary social services, and the right to security in the event of unemployment, sickness, disability, widowhood, old age or other lack of livelihood in circumstances beyond his control."

Mid-twentieth-century international institutions such as the United Nations, the World Bank, and the International Monetary Fund (IMF) have offered assistance and hope but with mixed success. The World Bank and IMF particularly have sometimes, and with justifiable concern to prevent corruption, attached such stringent fiscal conditions and economic straitjackets on recipient nations that those most in need cannot possibly qualify. The new world of the twenty-first century may require entirely new financial lending institutions to meet the old needs and new realities of our time.

Further, preoccupation with the terrorist threat from the Islamic world cannot so mesmerize the United States that it neglects festering social conditions to our south, in Latin America, and congenital inequalities in Africa. One senior retired U.S. military officer identified the greatest threat to America as "unemployed eighteen- to thirty-five-year-old males worldwide."

The struggle for global human rights will cost the United States and its developed democratic allies far less than the cost of maintaining vast military structures to protect ourselves from the consequences of despair. Some, for fanatical ideological reasons, will still choose to attack us even were this goal to be achieved. But they would, at the very least, encounter considerable more difficulty in locating troubled waters in which to swim and plot treachery if hope and opportunity were the worldwide standard.

The goal of the expansion of rights, political and humanitarian, will require "preventive diplomacy," the anticipation of conflict before it arises and becomes a threat and the implementation of therapeutic steps to alleviate alienation and despair. This task will test American statecraft, the ability to exercise economic and political power in the interest of common humanity.

The concept of statecraft itself is not commonly understood and is often mistaken for traditional diplomacy. Yet statecraft is a more nuanced and complex notion. It requires its adherents to consider not only their own national interests but to see as well the interests of others through their eyes and to seek ways to accommodate both.

Statecraft, diplomacy at its highest level, must be the standard to which the United States, as mature democracy and world leader, aspires. United States statecraft must be placed at the service of human aspirations and become a central hallmark of America's political leadership. In selecting its leaders and in considering how to achieve future security, Americans will soon realize that those with the rare gift of statecraft are to be preferred above all others.

Emerging Powers and Shared Responsibilities

America can either hoard power, shoulder disproportionate security responsibilities, and suffer the loss of lives and resources, or it can empower others to assume roles as security guarantors in our common interests.

The United States must endeavor to encourage at least three major nations, India, China, and Russia, to assume an increasing share of regional security responsibilities. The potential for friction between the United States and each of these nations will decrease as each of them accepts security partnerships with the United States and other allies to deal with potential conflicts and threats in their respective regions. Likewise, America's traditional allies in Europe must be strongly urged to resume a greater role within the liberal democratic

> America can either hoard power, shoulder disproportionate security responsibilities, and suffer the loss of lives and resources, or it can empower others to assume roles as security guarantors in our common interests.

community for local, regional, and global security.

The United States need not share everything in common with other nations in order to share an interest in and responsibility for security. In each case, the United States has differences with Russia, China, and India. These differences are managed through diplomatic and political channels whether bilaterally or through international organizations. In the case of Russia and China, differences have provided the occasion for friction. A certain degree of bilateral friction is normal between powerful nations, but much is unnecessary. Some in the United States have sought to maximize differences and demonize one or both of those countries. For example, as recently as March 2006, a Council on Foreign Relations task force report, "Russia's Wrong Directions," concluded that in every instance of friction between the United States and Russia, Russia was at fault.[6]

The result of this parochial thinking in the case of Russia particularly is to strengthen the hands of Russian nationalists and those who respond adversely to what they perceive to be denigration of Russian sovereignty and promotion of American hegemony.

We accept healthy national competitiveness. As with strong-willed and ambitious individuals, much of this competition among nations is natural. But Russia experiences no benefit from America's adversities nor do we draw benefit from theirs. India is the largest democracy in Asia and a stabilizing force. China is our creditor, supplier, and market and can lend considerable weight in the resolution of North Korea's nuclear ambitions. A renegade North Korea is a greater danger to China's security than it is to ours. Properly and skillfully engaged, Russia can be a critical bridge between Europe and Asia. It can play an instrumental role in negotiating limits on Iran's nuclear operations, and it is strategically located on the borders of several Islamic republics. Its size, location, and resources guarantee its strategic importance and its continuing significance in world affairs.

We were critical of Russia's military operations in Chechnya until we found ourselves occupied in two brutal insurgencies in Asia and the Middle East. Russia has not progressed into liberal democracy nearly as quickly as we had somewhat casually assumed it would. There are many historical and cultural reasons for this. But our eastward expansion of NATO, an anti-Soviet security alliance for forty years, nearer to Russia's borders, our deployment of ballistic missile defenses near its borders, and our offer of very minimal assistance in its efforts to construct a civil society have not helped. We have a number of important economic and political interests in common with Russia, among them a common interest in security, our interest in its oil, a mutual interest in stabilizing its former Islamic republics, our interest in Russia as a market for American products and services, and the importance of Russia as a cooperative ally in the Middle East and elsewhere. For unclear reasons, policy makers in both American parties have chosen to alienate if not demonize Russia. This is neither in our interest nor in Russia's.

Likewise, until the outbreak of the war on terrorism, some U.S. officials and ideological factions favored an extremely hard line where China was concerned. This bias neglected our growing need for Chinese credit to finance our large deficits, our interest in China's markets, our importation of vast amounts of Chinese products, and our need for China's cooperation in stabilizing its region. As with Russia, other than the need for an antagonist against whom to rally American public opinion, the source of this latent American belligerence is obscure.

There are, unfortunately, those in the foreign policy arena, some in high places, who operate from the principle that America requires an enemy or a conflict. Otherwise, for them, how else to unify the American people and thus govern the country? How else to justify continuing historically huge military

> There are, unfortunately, those in the foreign policy arena, some in high places, who operate from the principle that America requires an enemy or a conflict.

budgets? How else to gain consensus for new weapons systems and nuclear "modernization"? If one's world view is that life is a Hobbesian jungle, with political nature red in tooth and claw, then a world at relative peace becomes an unsettling thing.

With regard to Russia, China, and a number of other regional powers, a different view of human nature, one with a more hopeful view of human flourishing, the common good, and the common interest, must prevail. Otherwise, we are in for a very difficult century.

We make no compromise of our own principles, or our own security, by exploring common cause and resolving tensions with these regional powers. By sharing responsibilities for security in their regions we empower them, bind them closer to us, and demonstrate the mutual advantages of cooperation. Our powerful stance on behalf of the principles of democracy is not sufficient reason for us to exclude those who do not meet our standards. There is considerable difference between encouraging democracy and demanding democracy as a condition for cooperative relations. The security of the global commons will be achieved by different nations with different political systems, traditions, and cultures engaging in this common pursuit. Having George Washington as a founding president is not a condition for desiring a more secure world.

There are a number of examples of how a new round of security internationalism can make us safer. For instance, serious consideration should be given by the

United States to creation of an Asian Treaty Organization patterned after NATO and involving Japan, China, South Korea, and the United States, as an adjunct to the existing Southeast Asian Treaty Organization (SEATO).

Similarly, cooperative security arrangements with other influential regional powers should be cultivated. Brazil, Mexico, Turkey, and Indonesia, along with Egypt, Pakistan, and possibly South Africa, are important nations with whom close security ties are mutually and collectively beneficial. But, like individual friendships, these ties cannot be taken for granted. Nor can they be seen to benefit the United States alone. In the past, too often we have sought the help of other nations when it was in our interest to do so. Our security relations must increasingly be based on shared interests and mutual benefits.

Two contradictory international forces, integration through globalization and disintegration, will dominate the early twenty-first century. The forces of disintegration may cause the failure of states, permeate regions of Africa, Asia, and the Middle East, permit the privatization of pollution by corporate interests, encourage primitivism and tribalism, subvert order, promote ignorance and insecurity, and cloak power in ignorance, dogma, and mystery. The forces of integration are interweaving national economies, coordinating environmental actions, strengthening governance, spreading technology, increasing transparency, expanding information, and meshing security.

Creating a global commons of liberal democracies must not represent a rejection of the rest of the world. The sixty or so progressive democracies should not band together for the purpose of turning our backs on the remaining 130 or so nations. This would be a prescription for unnecessary global division, conflict, and instability.

Attention must also be paid to the increasing gap between haves and have-nots within emerging regional powers. India has evolved a large middle class, but one that is still outweighed by the vast majority in poverty. Likewise, with dramatic speed in the last fifteen years China has created a huge consumer class. But, like Russia, prosperity is largely confined to the largest cities, and hundreds of millions remain at or near mere subsistence levels. Great disparity of income in these and other nations must be of great concern to them and to the rest of the world as a growing source of unrest that could lead to internal conflict and regional instability.

It is critical to the security of the commons that nations such as Russia, China, and India, as well as other regional powers mentioned above, be included in the world of integration rather than the world of disintegration. Increased integration does not decrease competition, but competition is not a threat to security. International integration does not solve all problems. The twenty-first-century challenge is to manage those problems that cannot be solved and to identify more with what unites us than what divides us.

As a first resort in conflict resolution, force represents a diminishing return. Military power, and the willingness to use it, will remain a crucial deterrent to rogue states. But the United States cannot insist on a monopoly in deterrence and will increasingly find it useful and effective to cooperate with others in maintaining order and keeping peace.

Part III. A New Definition of Strength

The Tyranny of Oil:
Energy as Central to America's Security Strategy

America's continuing dependency on oil from the Persian Gulf is its greatest source of vulnerability and therefore its greatest weakness. Our economic foundations and thus our national security are held hostage to this dependency.

The United States cannot be secure if it continues to be dependent on unstable supplies of foreign oil. Oil is now the centerpiece of America's foreign policy, economic policy, defense policy, environmental policy, and energy policy. Our major policy concerns must be liberated from oil dependency if the United States is to restore its credibility, authority, and integrity in the world.

Total independence from international oil supplies is not a realistic national objective. The United States imports over 60 percent of the oil it consumes from abroad. Some authoritative estimates place that number nearer 70 percent within the next twenty years. A number of major suppliers, such as Mexico and Canada, are stable and predictable. Others, such as Venezuela and Russia, are less dependable and use their oil supplies for political leverage. By far, however, the most dangerous dependency is located in large portions of the Persian Gulf.

Much has been made of our addiction to oil. But the consequences of that addiction have not been sufficiently understood. The addict's behavior is characterized by this: abandonment of principle. Standards of conduct, sober practices, and noble ideals are cast aside under the relentless and demonic urges of addiction. This is true of nations as well as individuals. Our first principle is that we are a democratic republic. Yet, under the relentless thirst for oil, we are engaged in conduct more characteristic of an empire, and an especially greedy one at that.

The United States has engaged in two Gulf Wars in a decade and a half and has been embroiled in its second Gulf War for almost five years. Despite extreme reluctance on the part of our leaders to be candid, few believe oil has nothing to do with these wars. The Persian Gulf is the most unstable region of the world. Every diplomatic effort must be made to bring peace to this troubled region, and the good offices of our allies must be brought to bear as well. Despite maximum attention and engagement, however, stable governments and stable relations in the Middle East will remain a difficult objective for the United States to achieve. But they will be impossible for us to achieve so long as our every motive is made suspect by our unquenchable thirst for oil from that region.

Therefore, America's security requires that we become sufficiently independent of that portion of our imported oil coming from the Persian Gulf so that, if our access to it is denied, we are not forced to engage in war to obtain it. Security is not achievable under the conditions of dependency. Dependency, in this case on the oil supplies of others, guarantees vulnerability. Oil is fungible. Persian Gulf oil enters world markets and has no distinguishing characteristics. Nevertheless, we can have as our national security goal to reduce our imports by roughly 20 to 25 percent, representing the quantity that comes from that region. This would have the therapeutic effect also of substantially reducing our huge trade deficit.

Our vulnerability has led to the compromise of our principles. Even as we have insisted that our war in Iraq

is to bring democracy to the Middle East, we have supported oligarchies, dictators, and
repressive governments in this
region because we depend on
their oil. A great nation will not
permit oil to make it a hypocrite
in the eyes of the world. We must
not let oil addiction continue to

> We must not let oil addiction
> continue to force us to aban-
> don our most cherished beliefs
> and principles. And we abso-
> lutely must not sacrifice the
> lives of our sons and daughters
> so that we may drive ineffi-
> cient, wasteful vehicles.

force us to abandon our most cherished beliefs and principles. And we absolutely must not sacrifice the lives of
our sons and daughters so that we may drive inefficient,
wasteful vehicles.

The world's economy is heavily dependent on an
intricate network of oil supplies and distribution. As
the U.S. Commission on National Security concluded in
September 1999, "the stability of the world oil market will
continue to depend on the uninterrupted supply of oil
from the Persian Gulf ... "[7] This conclusion recognizes
the danger that major interruption of those supplies could
cripple the globalized network of consumers and producers. This reality does not assume, as previous leaders have,
that it necessarily requires the United States to be the
default guarantor of those oil supply networks.

The United States must consider organizing an international consortium of oil consuming nations—it might be
called the Organization of Petroleum Importing Nations
(OPIN)—to collectively guarantee the continued flow of
oil supplies, from the Persian Gulf particularly, if political
instability threatens them. Such an organization would, of
course, require the approval and compliance of regional oil
producers in whose economic interest it would be to have
continued production and distribution guaranteed.

To further remove the United States from its current
role as default guarantor of world oil supplies, we might
urge the United Nations, also in cooperation with oil

producing states in the region and to avoid charges of de facto U.S. imperialism, to consider declaring the Persian Gulf region a Zone of International Interest and provide an official mandate to an organization composed of oil producing and oil consuming nations to guarantee continued oil supplies to ensure stability of world markets regardless of political conditions prevailing in the region.

To the degree that the United States requires a military presence in the region, it need not be in the form of land-deployed forces of the sort that inspired the deadly Khobar Towers attack on U.S. forces barracked there. Formidable carrier task groups, including squadrons of air superiority fighter and attack aircraft, can be kept on station "over the horizon" in case an American military force is required to help prevent attacks on oil production and distribution facilities in the region. As a maritime nation dependent on ocean highways for commerce and security and in an age when occupation triggers suicidal resistance, America's naval capabilities take on increased importance and responsibility.

As an operating capability, an international collection of special forces trained and equipped to maintain oil production and distribution might be created, under U.S. leadership, to ensure that conflict, unrest, or terrorist attacks do not deny the global economy the oil it requires. This will become increasingly important as major new economies, such as India and China, grow and expand their demand for oil. International guarantees of this sort, and the capability for underwriting them, will also be critical if major suppliers experience domestic turmoil or civil war.

It is no longer acceptable for American economic and political security to be held hostage by its addiction to fragile oil supplies, an addiction that requires warfare to satisfy it. Our unnecessary dependencies have compromised our well-being and that of future generations, the integrity of our foreign policy, and our very constitutional principles and ideals. No other single measure so requires our attention and our immediate action as the urgency of liberation from dangerous oil dependency. Opinions differ as to degrees of political stability among Persian Gulf oil producers. Not all experts share the view that oil producing states are fragile. An abundance of caution, however, requires us to consider the consequences, however remote, of political unrest, interrupted supplies, and economic dislocation caused by dramatic oil price spikes.

We are responsible for a certain portion of our vulnerability. Despite repeated direct and indirect suggestions of dialogue, we have chosen confrontation with Iran. Much of this approach flows from hostage taking of U.S. diplomats by revolutionary zealots angry at our support for the late shah and, even earlier, our overthrow of Iran's prime minister during the Cold War. History has its reckonings. Regardless, it is now very much in our interest to begin the long process of starting anew in reestablishing relations with a nation strategically placed to play a central role in determining whether the Middle East will, or will not, be a stable region.

Conservation and energy efficiency, especially in our transportation patterns and types of vehicles we use, are crucial to energy security. They are also central to reversal of another critical vulnerability: climate change.

Mandated fuel-efficiency standards, carbon taxes, renewable fuel supplies, advanced-technology engines, and composite automobile-fabrication methods are among the wide range of solutions to our unnecessarily wasteful addictions.

Our current policy is to rely on unstable supplies to fuel wasteful vehicles and to sacrifice the lives of our sons and daughters to get the oil if it is cut off. This policy is not only unnecessary, it is immoral. The historian Barbara

Tuchman defined folly on a national scale as the pursuit of a policy known to be flawed while a better alternative is acknowledged to exist.

This generation of Americans must not permit history to judge us as a generation that risked its security, and its moral authority, in pursuit of folly.

Thus, at the center of America's twenty-first-century security is independence from Persian Gulf oil supplies and formulation of a multinational treaty organization that guarantees oil will be supplied to the global economic commons. More than any other measures, these combined steps will restore the credibility and good faith of the United States and enable us to behave in accordance with the principles of our Constitution.

Economic Imagination:
The Base of America's Political Leadership

The security of the United States is totally dependent upon the security of its economy. National security as a purely military concept is, thus, too narrow. Military strength cannot be maintained without a sound financial basis. That basis can only be found in a sound dollar and an expanding economy. To possess a thriving economy in a revolutionary age is, of necessity, to be revolutionary. To be revolutionary in the early twenty-first century is to pioneer in knowledge and information and in their transmission and communication.

What began to dawn on a few younger political leaders thirty years ago or more now seems self-evident and irrefutable: the computer is the symbol of the age in which we live, as much as the steam engine was the symbol of the industrial age. Information and its cyber networks are transforming whole economies and entire regions. China and India today are much different countries than they were a mere fifteen years ago. Growing economies

are seldom threatening economies; economies networked
by trade relations are even less
so. Thus, as nations are able
to join the rapidly evolving
information world, any threats
to our security that they may

Growing economies are seldom threatening economies; economies networked by trade relations are even less so. Thus, as nations are able to join the rapidly evolving information world, any threats to our security that they may have represented subside.

have represented subside. Instead, these emerging economies represent competitive challenges to our dominance
in the new information age and thus challenges to the
economic base upon which our security rests.

To flourish in the information age, the United States
must invest. We must invest in research, in new technologies, in experimentation, in innovative equipment, and
most of all in the human mind. Not all citizens will be
pathfinding inventors. But all who hope for new opportunities must know how to use the inventions of the
pathfinders. A new Great Game is underway. It is not to
determine, as in the past, what power will dominate a particular geostrategic region of the globe. It is to determine
who will win the Game of Invention. This game is being
played out not on the playing fields or the battlefields,
but in the classrooms, laboratories, research centers, and
inner recesses of the inventive human mind.

"Second only to a weapon of mass destruction deto-
nating in an American city, we can think of nothing more
dangerous [to United States security] than a failure to
manage properly science, technology, and education for
the common good over the next quarter century."[8] This
dramatic but considered conclusion in the final report of
the U.S. Commission on National Security in early 2001
led to the recommendation that the U.S. government
double its investment in science and technology research
and development by 2010. Eight years later, tragically,
there has been no effort even to begin to reach this goal.

As a result, today our nation is less secure.

The linkages are both simple and inescapable. Military strength requires a productive economy. A productive twenty-first-century information-age economy requires constant renewal, reinvigoration, and advance. Renewal requires innovation and invention. Innovation requires investment. Because we are not investing, principally in the human mind, we are undermining our own national security and our ability to lead the world.

In more-normal times, where time is not urgent and competition is not intense, it might be sufficient to leave investment in innovation to the private sector. But financial markets measure success by very short-term standards. And in a dynamic and revolutionary age, the profit motive alone is not sufficient to guarantee the public resources necessary to achieve security. Of course, in our system of regulated markets, much of cutting-edge invention will emerge from private corporations eager to occupy if not also dominate new markets. This motivation will certainly help fuel economic expansion. But a private sector primarily focused on quarterly returns is not always eager to reinvest current profits in long-term research that will provide a return on investment only with the passage of years.

> Because we are not investing, principally in the human mind, we are undermining our own national security and our ability to lead the world.

Thus, quite often, as with space, jet engines, and futuristic medical technologies, high-risk, longer-reward research and development is dependent on public investment in the national, rather than the corporate, interest. Public and university research laboratories, not immediately dependent on short-term profits, have the advantage of speculative, trial-and-error latitude not always available to private researchers. Through tax incentives and patent policy, private investment in research can and must be encouraged. But it must be supplemented and often led by government-sponsored research and development aimed solely at United States economic leadership in the patterns of innovation necessary to guarantee our national security.

A creative, inventive economy is a growing economy. And a growing economy provides the resources for military power abroad and security of the homeland. Increasingly, however, the United States will find itself involved in collaborative advanced research that will benefit other nations as well. Some projects on the cutting edge of space, medicine, computer science, and advanced physics are too large for even the most dominant economy and too important for humankind to be monopolized by any single nation, including the United States. Like security itself, expensive, large-scale invention and innovation, such as the Large Hadron Collider (LHC) on the Swiss-French border, must increasingly be collaborative in nature. Just as security will increasingly be found on the global commons, so the advancement of knowledge will require its own information commons, an integrated international laboratory of research and learning.

> Some projects on the cutting edge of space, medicine, computer science, and advanced physics are too large for even the most dominant economy and too important for humankind to be monopolized by any single nation, including the United States.

Economic competition is dependent on Schumpeter's creative gales of destruction of the old and introduction of the new. Where introduction of the new is of universal benefit, however, competition will necessarily be joined by international collaboration. The age of information is eroding a previous century of secrecy. There are increasingly few secrets, and nothing is secret for very long. The United States is at a crossroads in the new information age. It can choose to go it alone in advanced research, in the interest of secrecy and national advantage, or it can open its doors and laboratories to the best minds of the planet and become the university and laboratory of the world.[9] Opportunities for permanent national advantage protected by secrecy are diminishing in the age of information. We can either hide our diminishing scientific secrets behind closed laboratory doors and national borders, or we can be the world's laboratory, sharing the inventions of collaborative international research. There will be occasions where we continue to pursue the former, but those occasions will diminish as the opportunities for the latter increase.

No more obvious instance of this principle exists than regarding space. The costs of space exploration are enormous, even by the standards of the dominant U.S. economy. But our economy is debt-ridden and dependent on borrowing from others, particularly China and Japan, and from our children. Very soon we will have no choice but to organize the advanced nations of the world to join in the space exploration venture. That it has taken us several decades to confront this reality will be a source of wonder to historians of the future. Internationally manned space shuttle crews are a great step in this direction.

Space does not belong to the United States any more than do the oceans of the world. Open sea-lanes of communication, unobstructed maritime straits and chokepoints, and protected fisheries are in the interest of the global commons. Those sharing this commons cooperate with us, sometimes through international treaties, sometimes without, to achieve these objectives and to sustain them. This model applies with even greater force to the interests of all humankind in free and open access to space, the prevention of an arms race in space, and in sharing the wonders of space exploration.

Innovation requires investment. America's economic

security cannot be guaranteed so long as we are increasingly a debtor nation. A debtor, by definition, is never secure. Even a powerful debtor knows that a cloud of interest and repayment follows it throughout the marketplace. We cannot claim to be secure or strong so long as we find it necessary to borrow from lenders such as the Chinese to finance both our debt and our military. We pay for the mightiest army in the world with borrowed money. This is perhaps our most sinister vulnerability.

> We pay for the mightiest army in the world with borrowed money. This is perhaps our most sinister vulnerability.

The soundness of the dollar is inextricably linked to our strength and our security. At this advanced stage of our national history it should be trite to remind ourselves of old adages such as "Do not spend what you have not earned." But remind ourselves we must.

The United States will always have its own national economic interests. It must look to the well-being and security of its own citizens first. In the globalized, networked, and integrated world of the twenty-first century, however, we will find that achieving our own national objectives by ourselves will prove increasingly problematic and that our national flourishing, our citizens' prosperity and aspirations, and even our national destiny will be inseparable from the flourishing, aspirations, and destiny of our fellow human beings.

This is the central aspect of the security of the commons. World leadership in the twenty-first century will be achieved by those who devise new ways to go it together, not go it alone. In the last century national security was in one category and economic policy in another. In this century they are inseparable. And economic strength now is contained in 300 million American minds, minds that require stimulation, imagination, enlargement, and possibility.

The American Nation:
A New Approach to Security at Home

The consolidation of federal agencies obligated to protect the American nation from terrorist attack occurred too late to prevent the catastrophe of September 11, 2001. Even now, eight years later, our nation is not as safe as it can be and should be.

The best standard for gauging preparedness, whether for terrorist attack or national disaster, is suggested by one of the nation's leading experts: *national resilience.* Resilience is the ease with which an individual or nation recovers from shock or attack. This standard provides measures for determining how quickly, efficiently, and effectively we can recover from either threat and how resilient our national public and private systems are. The standard of resilience considers the hardening of the critical infrastructure: financial, communications, transportation, and energy systems; the availability of redundancy in critical systems; response and recovery times; training and equipping of first responders; damage containment; and rapid support for victims.[10]

Having more than seven years' experience in attempting to structure homeland security, it is timely to reconsider what that phrase means and how it is to be achieved. Two points of view offer themselves. One says that the absence of another major attack proves that we are doing many things right. The other says that we have been fortunate and remain unnecessarily vulnerable. To some degree both are correct. But now, with a new administration, stock-taking requires that all policies be reviewed.

Almost a year after the September 11 attacks, our government finally consolidated twenty-two agencies, composed of 187,000 existing federal employees, under one new cabinet secretary responsible for homeland security. The department's badly flawed response to the

Hurricane Katrina disaster revealed serious problems in its structure and management. Many lessons learned from that failure provide an opportunity to reorganize the department along more effective and functional lines that will increase border and port security, prevent future attacks, provide prompt and effective response to attacks that are unavoidable, and train and equip local public safety responders who will be integrated with and provide support to the National Guard.

The department's focus on airport security at the expense of other vulnerable areas is increasingly misplaced. Too little progress has been made, for example, in the area of seaport and container shipping security, in preparation for biological attack, and in integration of U.S. Coast Guard and Customs and Border Protection databases and communications systems.

Additionally, central to the restoration of public confidence in homeland security will be better management of federal-state and state-local cooperation. The federal role in oversight of state and local expenditures on security projects must be substantially increased. Greater accountability by state and local governments and greater transparency in the way federal grants are allocated are required. Federal resources must be allocated according to threat likelihood and vulnerabilities and not based on traditional political considerations. Congress must refuse to continue to view homeland security as a source for political payouts, trading votes for local projects in order to gain reelection. The American people demand a higher standard from their elected representatives on a matter this close to the life and death of the nation.

Federal, state, and local coordination must be increased. Joint training, equipping, and emergency drilling must become the standard. In addition, the public must be informed on a regular basis of steps taken at every government level to enhance citizen and community security. Too little involvement of the public has encouraged both skepticism and complacency. A sense of citizen security is totally dependent on transparency and candor regarding our failures and weaknesses as well as our successes.

Reorganization of the Department of Homeland Security may also require it to become smaller and more focused. This national security strategy proposes a high-level review commission to make recommendations to the new administration for restructuring the department to maximize its effectiveness and focus and to recommend a new set of priorities based on most likely threats and most imperative response capabilities.

Most important, the National Guard, the backbone of domestic security, must be trained and equipped for and restored to that mission. The Constitution of the United States explicitly recognized the central role of the militia, the eighteenth-century forbearers of the National Guard, in defending the American nation. Article I, Section 8 includes this: "The Congress shall have Power.... to provide for organizing, arming, and disciplining the Militia," and the Second Amendment provides that "A well-regulated Militia, being necessary to the security of a free State, the right of the people to keep and bear Arms, shall not be infringed."

The philosophical reason for this constitutional recognition of the importance of citizen-soldiers springs from our character as a republic and the resistance by ancient and modern republican thinkers, including our own founders, to the notion of standing armies playing any political role in the life of the republic, especially in peacetime. The explicit provision for maintenance of a militia under state control until employed by the national government was to represent the frontline of defense of the homeland against foreign incursion until the standing army, if necessary, could be deployed.

Fearing the imposition on the liberties of a free republic by misguided political or military leaders, from the founders forward we have relied upon citizen-soldiers to fortify the laws of the United States, and, in an age rightly concerned with the dangers of terrorism, we must continue to do so. This is also the thinking more recently of the U.S. Commission on National Security for the 21st Century, which concluded: "We urge, in particular, that the National Guard be given homeland security as a primary mission, as the U.S. Constitution ordains."[11]

This new approach to protecting the American nation will also insist that interagency rivalries, especially between the Federal Bureau of Investigation and the Central Intelligence Agency, be eliminated as an impediment to national security. While primacy of the FBI domestically and the CIA internationally must be observed, intelligence critical to protecting American citizens in their homes and communities must be made available to the most concerned agencies and law enforcement services on an urgent basis. Bureaucratic interests must not be permitted to interfere with national security, especially in a globalized world where domestic and international arenas are less well defined and often overlap.

Homeland security is a dynamic, not a static, concept and goal. Its efficacy is a test of our complex federal system, requiring all levels of government, from Washington to the smallest community, to be actively engaged. Public officials at all levels must be held and must hold themselves accountable to those they are sworn to protect. Taxpayers and media alike are obliged

> Homeland security is a dynamic, not a static, concept and goal. Its efficacy is a test of our complex federal system, requiring all levels of government, from Washington to the smallest community, to be actively engaged.

to demand periodic accounting by those obliged to protect Americans and their families.

In the arena of securing our nation, we have no choice but to become as effective at anticipation as we traditionally have been at reaction. One 9/11 attack is one too many. Defense of America's home supersedes all other security considerations. It is and must remain our highest priority. The realities of the day do not permit us to pick and choose among risks. Only the most tightly knit fabric of local and state first responders, National Guard, and national intelligence and law enforcement agencies at the peak of training and alertness is acceptable.

Our domestic security requires us to become a resilient nation, one that recovers from man-made or natural disasters promptly, efficiently, and with the least disruption to community and national life.

Military Innovation: Reform in the New Century

From one perspective human history represents either continuation of old patterns of conflict or evolution of new methods of violence, such as terrorists using civilian aircraft to carry out suicidal attacks on civilian targets. Either way, static defenses decline in effectiveness.

Facing new threats as well as new opportunities to preempt those threats, the United States must now fashion land, sea, and air forces trained and equipped for new missions. As nation-state wars decline, more unconventional and fourth-generation conflicts will emerge. Following generations of warfare featuring classic line-and-column tactics (mid-seventeenth to mid-nineteenth century), then attrition warfare (World War I), then maneuver warfare (World War II), fourth-generation warfare is characterized by the state's loss of a monopoly on violence, a return to a world of cultures, not nation-states, and the arrival of this new warfare by stateless nations on American soil.

All this was predicted well before September 11.[12]

These conflicts will require new military and para-military capabilities as well as new weapons and types of training. Increasingly our forces will cooperate with similar forces from allied nations. In addition to its traditional standing and reserve military forces, America's new military must include constabulary, nation strengthening, and civil-military capabilities.

The United States Commission on National Security for the 21st Century outlined five kinds of military forces our nation will require in the coming era. These include limited nuclear capabilities to deter and protect the United States and its allies from attack, homeland security capabilities, conventional forces necessary to win major wars, rapidly deployable expeditionary/intervention capabilities, and humanitarian relief and constabulary services.[13] But this same commission specifically addressed the homeland security mission in this way: "The National Guard—successor to the militia, and acknowledged in the Second Amendment as the historic defender of the Republic—must be trained and equipped to assume, among its other responsibilities, a significant role in defending the homeland in the 21st century."[14]

Almost twenty years after the end of the Cold War, reassessment of the role and size of our nuclear arsenal is well past due. Even during the Cold War it became redundant and excessive, with new warheads and delivery systems being added to, but not replacing, older systems in the inventory. Combined presidential and congressional commissions should review the size and structure of the nuclear arsenal, its security and deployment, and its mission and recommend substantial reductions in its components.

We face no peer nuclear competitor, and terrorists will not be deterred by our nuclear weapons. It is also highly questionable whether the use of nuclear weapons as a means of preventing proliferation, as in Iran, is an acceptable option given massive civilian casualty rates, the triggering of regional conflict, as in the Middle East, and the high moral cost of the United States being, yet again, the only nation to have used nuclear weapons in combat. The role of nuclear weapons as instruments of policy is highly limited. Any deterrent effect they may possess can be achieved with a fraction of the numbers now in our arsenal.

Given our continuing difficulties in Afghanistan and the downward-spiraling Iraqi civil war in which the U.S. occupying forces are embroiled, constabulary forces should be used only rarely and reluctantly. Our unilateral engagement in law enforcement, police training, and civil stabilization should be required only in those unique circumstances, such as Afghanistan, where our invading forces were justified in removing an immediate and unavoidable threat. As our founders repeatedly stated and as many subsequently have recalled, we alone are not and cannot be the policemen of the world.

The structure of our uniformed standing military forces reflects three and a half centuries of traditional nation-state warfare, including two world wars conducted with these force structures expanded on a massive scale. These structures include large army divisions divided into infantry, artillery, airborne, and motorized units, aircraft carrier task groups composed of a variety of surface and subsurface ships tasked with escorting and protecting the carrier centerpiece, and air wings and squadrons composed of bombers, fighters, and attack aircraft. Current structures also include mobile rapid-insertion forces, in the form of elements of the U.S. Marine Corps, and the several Special Forces, including the Rangers, Green Berets, Delta Force, Seals, and Air Force Special Forces. All combat units also require extensive support structures.

As some have proposed for the past two or three decades, the post–Cold War security needs of the United States now require force restructuring. Land forces must be increasingly organized around smaller units of battalion, brigade, and regimental size. They must be lighter, swifter, and more lethal, with less support "tail" and more point-of-the-spear "teeth." Naval forces must increasingly possess the capability of putting these lighter ground-combat forces ashore with faster and lighter landing craft, and they must be capable of patrolling coastal waters with lighter, swifter patrol boats. Long-range bomber missions and aerial combat dogfights will decline, and close air support of rapid-insertion forces will increase.

In the twenty-first century all U.S. military forces must be characterized by stealth, speed, range, unprecedented accuracy, lethality, and strategic mobility and must be guided by superior intelligence. The role of the Marines and Special Forces will increase. As the potential for prolonged conflict between massed nation-state armies declines, the potential for unconventional, irregular, local conflicts increases. And our contribution to international nation-stabilizing and disintegration management will require us to increase our civilian-military, constabulary, and peace-keeping capabilities in conjunction with other nations.

> In the twenty-first century all U.S. military forces must be characterized by stealth, speed, range, unprecedented accuracy, lethality, and strategic mobility and must be guided by superior intelligence.

As force structures are reformed in an era when the very nature of conflict is changing, so too the kinds of weapons these new forces require must be changed. Constant revolution in weapons technology and the sensors and guidance systems that control them make the platforms from which they operate—ships, planes, and tanks—obsolete if the two are inseparably integrated. Even though weapons and sensors advance rapidly, expensive platforms are built to last, in the case of aircraft carriers for as long as a half-century.

Therefore, it is a principle of reform of a high-tech military that weapons and sensor suites be capable of being lifted off, or "unplugged," from much longer-lasting air, sea, and land platforms, not only to save money but also to permit constant adjustment to technological innovation.

We must also consider creation of a new special force, one designed explicitly to protect the information technology systems at the core of our new economy. As important as highways and railroads were to manufacturing-based economies in the nineteenth and twentieth centuries, now cyber communications systems are even more important to our information-based economy in the twenty-first century. And these systems are even more vulnerable to attack by evildoers than our transportation systems have been.

A new Cyber Protective Corps, whether in uniform or not, must be tasked with guaranteeing the integrity of our critical infrastructure—the networks of finance, communications, energy, and transportation—upon which our twenty-first-century economy is based. High-tech assassins can cripple the U.S. economy without firing a shot or shedding a drop of blood. We are unprepared to deter or respond to a major

> High-tech assassins can cripple the U.S. economy without firing a shot or shedding a drop of blood. We are unprepared to deter or respond to a major assault on these systems.

assault on these systems. Even more dangerous is the ability of those not even within our borders to sabotage our information systems. The centerpiece of al Qaeda's doctrine is to cripple or destroy the American economy. Cyber systems are not protected by the Coast Guard, Customs and Border Protection, or other security assets.

Advanced knowledge-based economies must integrate a variety of national systems for protecting cyberspace.

The integration of our finance and communication systems with those of other nations around the globe means that our economic well-being can be severely undermined by those beyond our borders. All vulnerable, information-based national economies must collaborate to construct defenses against cyber assassins. Even if the United States developed foolproof barriers to protect its national systems from domestic attacks, our nation would remain vulnerable to attacks from abroad. There is no "national security" from cyber attacks.

> All vulnerable, information-based national economies must collaborate to construct defenses against cyber assassins.

This is an arena where other nations such as Russia and China, who may not always share our international agenda, have a common interest in banding together to protect our increasingly integrated economies from attacks that could damage all equally. The global cyber commons offers a new arena in which to seek integrated security in a world of new threats.

Strategically, the United States is a maritime power. We have friendly neighbors north and south and massive ocean-protected borders east and west. Our maritime forces represent our most flexible and maneuverable military asset. They require ports but no foreign bases. They are not occupying forces. In trouble spots such as the Persian Gulf, they can be kept over the horizon in the Indian Ocean and can cruise at will on the ocean highways. Carrier aircraft can project power ashore when required to do so, and expeditionary landing forces can be disembarked, supported, and protected from the air and the sea.

Among other duties, the United States Navy will continue to play a vital role, in cooperation with allied nations, in guaranteeing the trading world's access to sea-lanes of communication and critical straits and choke points. We are the world's greatest maritime power, and it is in our strategic interest to remain so.

Acknowledging the emerging imperative of combined and collaborative forces, the new chairman of the Joint Chiefs of Staff, Admiral Mike Mullen, recently applied this principle to his own service, the U.S. Navy. According to the *New York Times*, "Hints of an important initiative can be seen in Admiral Mullen's approach to how big a fleet the nation should buy. On his watch, the navy counts more than 270 ships, and the service set a goal of increasing to more than 300. But Admiral Mullen envisions putting to sea 'a thousand-ship navy'—a number he could arrive at by building relations with friendly nations whose vessels would sail as partners." ["Meeting Today's Military Demands, With an Eye on Tomorrow's," Thom Shanker, *New York Times*, September 30, 2007]

Even as our defense forces are reformed, restructured, and expanded into new security arenas, there is the critical question of when, where, and how U.S. military forces should be committed. To avoid ad hoc and reactive commitment of forces, this national security strategy establishes specific standards and conditions:

First, American military forces must be used to protect our security interests and those of our allies.

Second, we must clearly define what we are trying to accomplish, what our political and military objectives are. We must insist on tangible, obtainable political goals stated in concrete terms.

Third, the American people must support the use of their army and other forces in any sustained military operation, and they must be fully cognizant of proposed levels of military force and the potential costs, including of human lives.

Fourth, we should commit our forces only after diplomatic, political, and other means of conflict resolution have been exhausted and local forces are determined to be inadequate to resolve the conflict.

Fifth, we must be clear on how we intend to achieve our objectives and what strategies, tactics, and doctrines we mean to employ.

Sixth, we must have concurrence on the command structure of any military engagement and insist that the role of civilians who make policy not overlap the uniformed commanders tasked with carrying it out.

Seventh, the proposed operation and our thinking about it must pass the test of simplicity. The plan of operation must be achievable in its execution.

Every commander in chief must have always in mind that the army (and all military forces) belong to the people. If the people are deceived in the true purposes for committing our forces, any military operation will ultimately fail. Public support is critical to sustain military operations abroad. That support is totally dependent on accurate intelligence and leadership candor. As evidenced by public support for military operations in Iraq, even after the original justifications for invasion proved inaccurate or false, the American people were trusting and patient. But only up to a point. Once convinced that political leadership has been misguided, deceptive, and/or inept, public support will continue for the forces, but not for the mission.

It is now a matter for considerable concern that a measurable gap has opened between the people and the army, between citizens and warriors.[15] The all-volunteer force does not represent a cross section of America, and most Americans take their military service personnel for granted. "Support the troops" became a replacement for "stay the course" in political jargon and had little to do with the troops and much to do with continuation of a failed political course in Iraq. If the army belongs to the people, the people must take a direct interest in it. Civic education in a republic requires citizens to know what the military can, and cannot, do, how it operates and what it requires, and when it should, and should not, be deployed. And if political leadership misuses the military, it must pay a heavy political price.

Changing times require changing capabilities. It is a mistake to believe that the defenses of the past are adequate for a new and different age. Reorganization of the United States' regular military forces does not suggest that they will be any less needed for our national security. It simply means they will continue to be needed but for different tasks, roles, and missions. To resist change and accommodation to new realities is, as Thomas Jefferson wrote, to suggest that a man may continue to put on a coat that suited him as a boy.

Future security leadership will rest with those nations that grasp the rapidly changing nature of conflict, that can see over the horizon, and that adapt their security capabilities most quickly to respond to new realities. This is a restatement of Colonel John Boyd's formulation for all conflict: orientation, observation, decision, and action—the famous "OODA Loop."[16]

Conclusion
Resisting Hegemony without Seeking Hegemony

Hegemony is another word for dominance. The United States does not require hegemony to be secure.

By sharing security authority and responsibility, by founding our policies upon our constitutional principles and democratic republican traditions and heritage, and by considering the good of the global commons, the United States will once again be seen as a strong but benign power, one that seeks no empire, and one that deals openly and honestly with all humankind.

The early years of the twenty-first century found the United States on the threshold of empire. The justice of our cause in deposing the Taliban in Afghanistan was virtually unchallenged and unquestioned. It is a just war that now requires utmost international commitment to prosecute and successfully complete.

The lessons of the invasion and occupation of Iraq, on the contrary, are many and will take years to soberly contemplate and hopefully learn from. It is not too soon to conclude, however, that the underlying (and unstated) theory of the war was fatally flawed. Its advocates believed, though were reluctant to disclose, that we could use a post-Saddam Iraq, with a government favorably disposed toward continued American political and military influence, to settle conflicts in the Middle East on our terms. The Iraqis proved not to be so disposed and instead used their American-provided freedom from Saddam's yoke to reopen ancient grievances, to settle antique scores, and to vent their wrath on our occupation forces. More important, our strategy was imperialist in its conception.

This idea's advocates were well advised not to disclose it candidly. They had at least a primitive sense that the American people would not accept it. The inventors of the Iraq adventure would not be straightforward for the simple reason that from our founding, we have resisted empire.

It is plausibly argued that our expansion across the American continent, much of it accomplished by international treaties, was an imperial venture. There is something to this. Even so, however, one requires considerable imagination to equate the westward expansion on this continent with a policy of imperial hegemony in the most troubled region of the world characterized by historic tribal cultures, millennia-old religious strife, oligarchies, and colonially imposed, artificial national boundaries.

This is especially true when the central purpose of the enterprise was to secure the unacknowledged treasure of an energy-dependent global power: oil. Absent painful candor about purpose and motive, few profitable lessons will be learned from this tragically flawed and failed project, and its bitter pains will be suffered by future generations.

Put directly, our oil dependency is tempting us to become what we must not be. We pledge our allegiance to the flag of a republic founded by those who knew the true meaning of a republic. That knowledge was the foundation for their individual and collective insistence, repeatedly announced, that we must and would reject foreign entanglements. Knowing the essential nature of a republic, our founders possessed an abiding wisdom and intuitive sense that imperial ambition had the greatest chance to destroy our republic.

Resistance to hegemonic influence does not require that we isolate ourselves from a shrinking and increasingly interconnected world. Quite the contrary. It is a central premise of this national security strategy that we resist the hegemonic temptations of others. We should do so because we witnessed and were forced to resist early-twentieth-century ambitions of imperialism in Europe, mid-twentieth-century fascist aggressions in Europe and Asia, and later communist expansionism by other major powers. The costs were considerable. Therefore, we wish no future hegemonic ambitions, ideological or political, to take root.

Resisting hegemony, however, need not be a mission undertaken by the United States unilaterally. It is in the interest of many other nations that they also not experience, in much more direct ways in most cases than we, the influence of a hegemon. The security of the commons, a central premise of this national security strategy, presumes shared security burdens and multinational participation. A security strategy based upon the concept of resisting hegemony will attract many adherents. Few nations desire to be dominated. Virtually all would readily accept a role, commensurate with their means and assets as well as the dangers they face, in resisting domination.

Too often in recent years a false choice between internationalism and isolationism is posed by those who then argue that internationalism fails on the perfidy and weakness of our allies and isolation reduces the United States to a passive target for evildoers. The conclusion drawn is that the United States has no choice but to anticipate dangers and preempt them by eliminating evil in the world, to demonstrate willingness to use force before it is required in order to awe nations that may not even yet wish us ill, and to impose our will on contentious regions where any shadow over our national interest, a euphemism in many instances for oil, is cast.

This national security strategy does not assume animosity toward us before it is demonstrated. In recent post–Cold War years some have argued that China is a necessary competitor if not enemy. The facts are otherwise. China is our largest creditor, meaning that it believes in the underlying soundness of our economy, as well as one of our large and expanding markets. It defies logic to believe that China lends us much of its savings even as it plots our destruction. As with individuals, nations may provoke friction if they wish to. If we choose to alienate China and make it an enemy, much to our own detriment, we may do so. But such folly could only be embraced by those who are uncomfortable in a world without large enemies.

There has been a pattern in recent decades for our foreign policy to be at variance with our defense policy. This contest, or even competition, is no longer affordable. Our foreign and defense policies must be closely integrated. Our foreign policy and diplomacy must be robust, and our defense policy must be geared to threat reduction. Diplomacy is not the enemy of strength, nor is strength a substitute for diplomatic engagement. A new president will see that the Department of State and the Department of Defense are close partners coordinating their actions and are not competitors elbowing each other for supremacy over policy.

As ever, our national security will be based upon our greatest strength, our constitutional principles. We seek engagement with nations and peoples of good will in our common interest. This engagement requires of us humility, deference where due, and candor. Even more, it requires integrity and honor, the true sources of our moral authority and our qualification to lead.

> As ever, our national security will be based upon our greatest strength, our constitutional principles.

Enlightened engagement seeking common interest is our central principle. The United States has no need to manufacture enemies to remain on guard. We are intelligent enough and resourceful enough to know who among the family of nations to trust and who not to trust.

Our principle is engagement. Our method is cooperation. Our instincts are to seek the common good. Our belief is in strength through shared purpose.

—Gary Hart
New America Foundation

Endnotes

1. The Princeton Project, "Forging a World of Liberty under Law: U.S. National Security in the 21st Century," September 27, 2006.

2. U.S. Commission on National Security for the 21st Century, "Road Map for National Security: Imperative for Change," March 2001. This report, the most comprehensive of its kind since 1947, remains relevant to current national security policy. Of its fifty specific recommendations for enhancing U.S. national security, only one, the creation of a Department of Homeland Security, has been adopted as of 2009.

3. U.S. Commission on National Security for the 21st Century, "Seeking a National Strategy: A Concert for Preserving Security and Promoting Freedom," second report, April 15, 2000.

4. U.S. Commission on National Security for the 21st Century, "New World Coming," first report, September 15, 1999, 7.

5. Robert A. Pape, *Dying to Win: The Strategic Logic of Suicide Terrorism* (New York: Random House), 2005.

6. Council on Foreign Relations, "Russia's Wrong Directions," task force report, March 2006.

7. "New World Coming," 5.

8. "Road Map for National Security," 29.

9. National Academy of Sciences, "Science and Security," task force report, October 2007.

10. Steven Flynn, *The Edge of Disaster: Rebuilding a Resilient Nation* (New York: Random House), 2007.

11. U.S. Commission on National Security for the 21st Century, final report, January 2001.

12. Gary Hart, *The Shield & the Cloak: The Security of the Commons* (Oxford: Oxford University Press), 2006.

13. U.S. Commission on National Security for the 21st Century, "Roadmap for National Security."

14. U.S. Commission on National Security for the 21st Century, "Seeking a National Security Strategy," 15.

15. Kristin Henderson, "Their War," *Washington Post*, July 22, 2007.

16. William S. Lind, *Maneuver Warfare Handbook* (Boulder, Colo.: Westview Press), 1985.

Appendix I

Summary of the National Security Strategy: 2009

America's new national security strategy may be summarized in these conclusions:

The United States will act as the *watchman on the global tower*, alert to dangers on or just over the horizon of history and sharing warnings of those dangers as well as proposals for reducing them before they arise.

We will become the *principal guardian of the global commons*, undertaking to organize common responses to common challenges. We will seek to manage the opportunities of globalization while containing its risks.

The *architecture of common security* will be built upon a new concert of liberal democracies constructed around the notion of collaborative sovereignty and the ability of nations sharing common political values to act quickly and decisively when required to respond to dangers.

Those not currently in the liberal democratic fold will be welcomed into its common security and shared economic prosperity as they adopt liberal democratic institutions and practices.

Nation strengthening and nation restructuring will increasingly be a requirement for the stability of the global commons. Fragmentation into ethnic and religious stateless nations and enclaves must be resisted.

Peacemaking will preclude peacekeeping, and those stable nations of good will and common purpose will unite in enforcing the laws on the global commons.

Regional powers will be encouraged and invited to use their economic and political strength to pacify the regions they occupy in cooperation with other nations of good will, and they will find it increasingly to their advantage to do so.

America's military strength will increase through reform and restructuring of our military to meet new realities and challenges, and new types of forces will augment reformed traditional force structures.

The United States homeland will become more secure and resistant to attack by restructuring those governmental institutions at federal, state, and local levels dedicated to the prevention of foreign incursion and to the response to unavoidable attacks. The standard for homeland security will be national resilience.

Independence from unstable oil supplies from the Persian Gulf will become a centerpiece of America's national security and will enable us to avoid further wars in the Middle East even as we seek diplomatic and political solutions to its conflicts. In the interest of global economic stability, the task of guaranteeing the free flow of oil supplies will become an international obligation.

The United States now recognizes the imperative of investment in scientific innovation as the cornerstone of our economic, and therefore our national, security.

Together with the advanced nations of the world, we will explore for new ways to create opportunity and thus inspire hope for the majority of humans who currently possess neither.

It is the policy of the United States to resist hegemony without seeking hegemony for itself. We will pursue this course because it is required by our ancient republican heritage. This is our national security strategy.

Appendix II
"Road Map for National Security: Imperative for Change,
Executive Summary," The United States Commission
on National Security/21st Century, March 15, 2001

Executive Summary
A bipartisan commission set up to evaluate the current
national security climate and propose changes needed to
meet new threats has issued a report that calls for major
changes in governmental structures and processes.

Included in the report released January 31, 2001, by
the United States Commission on National Security/21st
Century are a proposal for a new, cabinet-level National
Homeland Security Agency that would combine the
Federal Emergency Management Agency with several
other agencies, and a prescription for recasting a "crippled" State Department and the Department of Defense.

The fourteen-member commission, headed by former
senators Gary Hart (D-CO) and Warren Rudman (R-
NH), includes other former legislators, Executive Branch
officials, military leaders, and representatives from business, academia, and the news media.

Following is the text of the executive summary of the
140-odd page report. The complete report can be accessed
at http://govinfo.library.unt.edu/nssg/PhaseIIIFR.pdf.
The website containing this document varies in slight, but
not material, degree from the original document.

Executive Summary

After our examination of the new strategic environment of the next quarter century (Phase I) and of a strategy to address it (Phase II), this Commission concludes that *significant changes must be made in the structures and processes of the U.S. national security apparatus.* Our institutional base is in decline and must be rebuilt. Otherwise, the United States risks losing its global influence and critical leadership role.

We offer recommendations for organizational change in five key areas:

- *ensuring* the security of the American homeland;
- *recapitalizing* America's strengths in science and education;
- *redesigning* key institutions of the Executive Branch;
- *overhauling* the U.S. government's military and civilian personnel systems; and
- *reorganizing* Congress's role in national security affairs.

We have taken a broad view of national security. In the new era, sharp distinctions between "foreign" and "domestic" no longer apply. We do not equate national security with "defense." We *do* believe in the centrality of strategy, and of seizing opportunities as well as confronting dangers. If the structures and processes of the U.S. government stand still amid a world of change, the United States will lose its capacity to shape history, and will instead be shaped by it.

Securing the National Homeland

The combination of unconventional weapons proliferation with the persistence of international terrorism will end the relative invulnerability of the U.S. homeland to catastrophic attack. A direct attack against American citizens *on American soil* is likely over the next quarter century. The risk is not only death and destruction but also a demoralization that could undermine U.S. global leadership. In the face of this threat, our nation has no coherent or integrated governmental structures.

We therefore recommend the creation of an independent National Homeland Security Agency (NHSA) with responsibility for planning, coordinating, and integrating various U.S. government activities involved in homeland security. NHSA would be built upon the Federal Emergency Management Agency, with the three organizations currently on the front line of border security—the Coast Guard, the Customs Service, and the Border Patrol—transferred to it. NHSA would not only protect American lives, but also assume responsibility for overseeing the protection of the nation's critical infrastructure, including information technology.

The NHSA Director would have Cabinet status and would be a statutory advisor to the National Security Council. The legal foundation for the National Homeland Security Agency would rest firmly within the array of Constitutional guarantees for civil liberties. The observance of these guarantees in the event of a national security emergency would be safeguarded by NHSA's interagency coordinating activities—which would include the Department of Justice—as well as by its conduct of advance exercises.

The potentially catastrophic nature of homeland attacks necessitates our being prepared to use the tremendous resources of the Department of Defense (DoD). Therefore, the department needs to pay far more attention to this mission in the future. *We recommend that a new office of Assistant Secretary for Homeland Security be created to oversee the various DoD activities in this domain and ensure that the necessary resources are made available.*

New priorities also need to be set for the U.S. armed forces in light of the threat to the homeland. *We urge, in particular, that the National Guard be given homeland security as a primary mission, as the U.S. Constitution itself ordains.* The National Guard should be reorganized, trained, and equipped to undertake that mission.

Finally, *we recommend that Congress reorganize itself to accommodate this Executive Branch realignment, and that it also form a special select committee for homeland security to provide Congressional support and oversight in this critical area.*

Recapitalizing America's Strengths in Science and Education

Americans are living off the economic and security benefits of the last three generations' investment in science and education, but we are now consuming capital. Our systems of basic scientific research and education are in serious crisis, while other countries are redoubling their efforts. In the next quarter century, we will likely see ourselves surpassed, and in relative decline, unless we make a conscious national commitment to maintain our edge.

We also face unprecedented opportunity. The world is entering an era of dramatic progress in bioscience and materials science as well as information technology and scientific instrumentation. Brought together and accelerated by nanoscience, these rapidly developing research fields will transform our understanding of the world and our capacity to manipulate it. The United States can remain the world's technological leader *if it makes the commitment to do so.* But the U.S. government has seriously underfunded basic scientific research in recent years. The quality of the U.S. education system, too, has fallen well behind those of scores of other nations. This has occurred at a time when vastly more Americans will have to understand and work competently with science and math on a daily basis.

In this Commission's view, the inadequacies of our systems of research and education pose a greater threat to U.S. national security over the next quarter century than any potential conventional war that we might imagine. American national leadership must understand these deficiencies as threats to national security. If we do not invest heavily and wisely in rebuilding these two core strengths, America will be incapable of maintaining its global position long into the 21st century.

We therefore recommend doubling the federal research and development budget by 2010, and instituting a more competitive environment for the allotment of those funds.

We recommend further that the role of the President's Science Advisor be elevated to oversee these and other critical tasks, such as the resuscitation of the national laboratory system and the institution of better inventory stewardship over the nation's science and technology assets.

We also recommend a new National Security Science and Technology Education Act to fund a comprehensive program to produce the needed numbers of science and engineering professionals as well as qualified teachers in science and math. This Act should provide loan forgiveness incentives to attract those who have graduated and scholarships for those still in school and should provide these incentives in exchange for a period of K–12 teaching in science and math, or of military or government service. Additional measures should provide resources to modernize laboratories in science education, and expand existing programs aimed at helping economically-depressed school districts.

Institutional Redesign

The dramatic changes in the world since the end of the Cold War have not been accompanied by any major institutional changes in the Executive Branch of the U.S. government. Serious deficiencies exist that only a significant organizational redesign can remedy. Most troublesome is the lack of an overarching strategic framework guiding U.S. national security policymaking and resource allocation. Clear goals and priorities are rarely set. Budgets are prepared and appropriated as they were during the Cold War.

The Department of State, in particular, is a crippled institution, starved for resources by Congress because of its inadequacies, and thereby weakened further. Only if the State Department's internal weaknesses are cured will it become an effective leader in the making and implementation of the nation's foreign policy. Only then can it credibly seek significant funding increases from Congress. The department suffers in particular from an ineffective organizational structure in which regional and functional policies do not serve integrated goals, and in which sound management, accountability, and leadership are lacking.

For this and other reasons, the power to determine national security policy has steadily migrated toward the National Security Council (NSC) staff. The staff now assumes policymaking roles that many observers have warned against. Yet the NSC staff's role as policy coordinator is more urgently needed than ever, given the imperative of integrating the many diverse strands of policymaking.

Meanwhile, the U.S. intelligence community is adjusting only slowly to the changed circumstances of the post-Cold War era. While the economic and political components of statecraft have assumed greater prominence, military imperatives still largely drive the analysis and collection of intelligence. Neither has America's overseas presence been properly adapted to the new economic, social, political, and security realities of the 21st century.

Finally, the Department of Defense needs to be over-hauled. The growth in staff and staff activities has created mounting confusion and delay. The failure to outsource or privatize many defense support activities wastes huge sums of money. The programming and budgeting process is not guided by effective strategic planning. The weapons acquisition process is so hobbled by excessive laws, regulations, and oversight strictures that it can neither recognize nor seize opportunities for major innovation, and its procurement bureaucracy weakens a defense industry that is already in a state of financial crisis.

In light of such serious and interwoven deficiencies, the Commission's initial recommendation is that *strategy should once again drive the design and implementation of U.S. national security policies.* That means that *the President should personally guide a top-down strategic planning process and that process should be linked to the allocation of resources throughout the government.* When submitting his budgets for the various national security departments, the President should also present an overall national security budget, focused on the nation's most critical strategic goals. Homeland security, counter-terrorism, and science and technology should be included.

We recommend further that the President's National Security Advisor and NSC staff return to their traditional role of coordinating national security activities and resist the temptation to become policymakers or operators. The NSC Advisor should also keep a low public profile. Legislative, press communications, and speechwriting functions *should reside in the White House staff, not separately in the NSC staff as they do today.* The higher the profile of the National Security Advisor the greater will be the pressures from Congress to compel testimony and force Senate confirmation of the position.

To reflect how central economics has become in U.S. national security policy, *we recommend that the Secretary of Treasury be named a statutory member of the National Security Council.* Responsibility for international economic policy should return to the National Security Council. *The President should abolish the National Economic Council, distributing its domestic economic policy responsibilities to the Domestic Policy Council.*

Critical to the future success of U.S. national security policies is a fundamental restructuring of the State Department. Reform must ensure that responsibility and accountability are clearly established, regional and functional activities are closely integrated, foreign assistance programs are centrally planned and implemented, and strategic planning is emphasized and linked to the allocation of resources.

We recommend that this be accomplished through the creation of five Under Secretaries with responsibility for overseeing the regions of Africa, Asia, Europe, Inter America, and Near East/South Asia, and a redefinition of the responsibilities of the Under Secretary for Global Affairs. The restructuring we propose would position the State Department to play a leadership role in the making and implementation of U.S. foreign policy, as well as to harness the department's organizational culture to the benefit of the U.S. government as a whole. Perhaps most important, the Secretary of State would be free to focus on the most important policies and negotiations, having delegated responsibility for integrating regional and functional issues to the Under Secretaries.

Accountability would be matched with responsibility in senior policymakers, who in serving the Secretary would be able to speak for the State Department both within the interagency process and before Congress. No longer would competing regional and functional perspectives immobilize the department. At the same time, functional perspectives, whether they be human rights, arms control, or the environment, will not disappear. The Under Secretaries would be clearly accountable to the Secretary of State, the President, and the Congress for ensuring that the appropriate priority was given to these concerns. Someone would actually be in charge.

We further recommend that the activities of the U.S. Agency for International Development be fully integrated into this new State Department organization. Development aid is not an end in itself, nor can it be successful if pursued independently of other U.S. programs and diplomatic activities. Only a coordinated diplomatic and assistance effort will advance the nation's goals abroad, whether they be economic growth, democracy, or human rights.

The Secretary of State should give greater emphasis to strategic planning in the State Department and link it directly to the allocation of resources through the establishment of a Strategic Planning, Assistance, and Budget Office. Rather than multiple Congressional appropriations, the State Department should also be funded in a single integrated Foreign Operations budget, which would include all foreign assistance programs and activities as well as the expenses for all related personnel and operations. Also, all U.S. Ambassadors, including the Permanent Representative to the United Nations, should report directly to the Secretary of State, and a major effort needs to be undertaken to "right-size" the U.S. overseas presence.

The Commission believes that the resulting improvements in the effectiveness and competency of the State Department and its overseas activities would provide the basis for the significant increase in resources necessary to carry out the nation's foreign policy in the 21st century.

As for the Department of Defense, resource issues are also very much at stake in reform efforts. The key to success will be direct, sustained involvement and commitment to defense reform on the part of the President, Secretary of Defense, and Congressional leadership. *We urge first and foremost that the new Secretary of Defense reduce by ten to fifteen percent the staffs of the Office of the Secretary of Defense, the Joint Staff, the military services, and the regional commands.* This would not only save money but also achieve the decision speed and encourage the decentralization necessary for any organization to succeed in the 21st century.

Just as critical, *the Secretary of Defense should establish a ten-year goal of reducing infrastructure costs by 20–25 percent through steps to consolidate, restructure, outsource, and privatize as many DoD support agencies and activities as possible.* Only through savings in infrastructure costs, which now take up nearly half of DoD's budget, will the department find the funds necessary for modernization and for combat personnel in the long-term.

The processes by which the Defense Department develops its programs and budgets as well as acquires its weapons also need fundamental reform. *The most critical first step is for the Secretary of Defense to produce defense policy and planning guidance that defines specific goals and establishes relative priorities.*

Together with the Congress, the Secretary of Defense should *move the Quadrennial Defense Review (QDR) to the second year of a Presidential term.* The current requirement, that it be done in an administration's first year, spites the purpose of the activity. Such a deadline does not allow the time or the means for an incoming administration to influence the QDR outcome, and therefore for it to gain a stake in its conclusions.

We recommend a second change in the QDR, as well; namely that the Secretary of Defense introduce a new process that requires the Services and defense agencies to compete for the allocation of some resources within the overall Defense budget. This, we believe, would give the Secretary a vehicle to identify low priority programs and begin the process of reallocating funds to more promising areas during subsequent budget cycles.

As for acquisition reform, the Commission is deeply concerned with the downward spiral that has emerged in recent decades in relations between the Pentagon as customer and the defense industrial base as supplier of the nation's major weapons systems. Many innovative high-tech firms are simply unable or unwilling to work with the Defense Department under the weight of its auditing, contracting, profitability, investment, and inspection regulations. These regulations also impair the Defense Department's ability to function with the speed it needs to keep abreast of today's rapid pace of technological innovation. Weapons development cycles average nine *years* in an environment where technology now changes every twelve to eighteen *months* in Silicon Valley—and the gap between private sector and defense industry innovation continues to widen.

In place of a specialized "defense industrial base," we believe that the nation needs a national industrial base for defense composed of a broad cross-section of commercial firms as well as the more traditional defense firms. "New economy" sectors must be attracted to work with the government on sound business and professional grounds; the more traditional defense suppliers, which fill important needs unavailable in the commercial sector, must be given incentives to innovate and operate efficiently. We therefore recommend these major steps:

- *Establish and employ a two-track acquisition system, one for major acquisitions and a "fast track" for a modest number of potential breakthrough systems, especially those in the area of command and control.*

- *Return to the pattern of increased prototyping and testing of selected weapons and support systems to foster innovation. We should use testing procedures to gain knowledge and not to demonstrate a program's ability to survive budgetary scrutiny.*

- *Implement two-year defense budgeting solely for the modernization element (R&D/procurement) of the Defense budget and expand the use of multi-year procurement.*

- *Modernize auditing and oversight requirements (by rewriting relevant sections of U.S. Code, Title 10, and the Federal Acquisition Regulations) with a goal of reducing the number of auditors and inspectors in the acquisition system to a level commensurate with the budget they oversee.*

Beyond other process reforms for the Defense Department, the Commission offers its suggestions on the force structure process. We conclude that the concept of two major, coincident wars is a remote possibility supported neither by the main thrust of national intelligence nor by this Commission's view of the likely future. It should be replaced by a new approach that accelerates the transformation of capabilities and forces better suited to the security environment that predominantly exists today. *The Secretary of Defense should direct the DoD to shift from the threat-based, force sizing process to one which measures requirements against recent operational activity trends, actual intelligence estimates of potential adversaries' capabilities, and national security objectives as defined in the new administration's national security strategy.*

The Commission furthermore recommends that *the Secretary of Defense revise the current categories of Major Force Programs (MFPs) used in the Defense Program Review to correspond to the five military capabilities the Commission prescribed in its Phase II report—strategic nuclear forces, homeland security forces, conventional forces, expeditionary forces, and humanitarian and constabulary forces.*

Ultimately, the transformation process will blur the distinction between expeditionary and conventional forces, as both types of capabilities will eventually possess enhanced mobility. For the near term, however, those we call expeditionary capabilities require the most emphasis. Consequently, *we recommend that the Defense Department devote its highest priority to improving and further developing its expeditionary capabilities.*

There is no more critical dimension of defense policy than to guarantee U.S. commercial and military access to outer space. The U.S. economy and military are vitally dependent on communications that rely on space. The clear imperative for the new era is a comprehensive national policy toward space and a coherent governmental machinery to carry it out. *We therefore recommend the establishment of an Interagency Working Group on Space (IWGS).*

The members of this interagency working group would include not only the relevant parts of the intelligence community and the State and Defense Departments, but also the National Aeronautics and Space Administration (NASA), the National Oceanic and Atmospheric Administration (NOAA), the Department of Commerce, and other Executive Branch agencies as necessary.

Meanwhile, the global presence and responsibilities of the United States have brought new requirements for protecting U.S. space and communications infrastructures, but no comprehensive national space architecture has been developed. *We recommend that such responsibility be given to the new interagency space working group and that the existing National Security Space Architect be transferred from the Defense Department to the NSC staff to take the lead in this effort.*

The Commission has concluded that the basic structure of the intelligence community does not require change. Our focus is on those steps that will enable the full implementation of recommendations found elsewhere within this report.

First in this regard, *we recommend that the president order the setting of national intelligence priorities through National Security Council guidance to the Director of Central Intelligence.*

Second, *the intelligence community should emphasize the recruitment of human intelligence sources on terrorism as one of its highest priorities, and ensure that existing operational guidelines support this policy.*

Third, *the community should place new emphasis on collection and analysis of economic and science/technology security concerns, and incorporate more open source intelligence into its analytical products.* To facilitate this effort, Congress should increase significantly the National Foreign Intelligence Program (NFIP) budget for collection and analysis.

The Human Requirements for National Security

As it enters the 21st century, the United States finds itself on the brink of an unprecedented crisis of competence in government. The declining orientation toward government service as a prestigious career is deeply troubling. Both civilian and military institutions face growing challenges, albeit of different forms and degrees, in recruiting and retaining America's most promising talent. This problem derives from multiple sources—ample private sector opportunities with good pay and fewer bureaucratic frustrations, rigid governmental personnel procedures, the absence of a single overarching threat like the Cold War to entice service, cynicism about the worthiness of government service, and perceptions of government as a plodding bureaucracy falling behind in a technological age of speed and accuracy.

These factors are adversely affecting recruitment and retention in the Civil and Foreign Services and particularly throughout the military, where deficiencies are both widening the gap between those who serve and the rest of American society and putting in jeopardy the leadership and professionalism necessary for an effective military. *If we allow the human resources of government to continue to decay, none of the reforms proposed by this or any other national security commission will produce their intended results.*

We recommend, first of all, a national campaign to reinvigorate and enhance the prestige of service to the nation. The key step in such a campaign must be to revive a positive attitude toward public service. This will require strong and consistent Presidential commitment, Congressional legislation, and innovative departmental actions throughout the federal government. It is the duty of all political leaders to repair the damage that has been done, in a high-profile and fully bipartisan manner.

From these changes in rhetoric, the campaign must undertake several actions. First, **this Commission recommends the most urgent possible streamlining of the process by which we attract senior government officials.** The ordeal that Presidential nominees are subjected to is now so great as to make it prohibitive for many individuals of talent and experience to accept public service. The confirmation process is characterized by vast amounts of paperwork and many delays. Conflict of interest and financial disclosure requirements have become a prohibitive obstacle to the recruitment of honest men and women to public service. Post-employment restrictions confront potential new recruits with the prospect of having to forsake not only income but work itself in the very fields in which they have demonstrated talent and found success. Meanwhile, a pervasive atmosphere of distrust and cynicism about government service is reinforced by the encrustation of complex rules based on the assumption that all officials, and especially those with experience in or contact with the private sector, are criminals waiting to be unmasked.

We therefore recommend the following:

- *That the President act to shorten and make more efficient the Presidential appointee process* by confirming the national security team first, standardizing paperwork requirements, and reducing the number of nominees subject to full FBI background checks.
- *That the President reduce the number of Senate-confirmed and non-career SES positions by 25 percent to reduce the layering of senior positions in departments that has developed over time.*
- *That the President and Congressional leaders instruct their top aides to report within 90 days of January 20, 2001 on specific steps to revise government ethics laws and regulations.* This should entail a comprehensive review of regulations that might exceed statutory requirements and making blind trusts, discretionary waivers, and recusals more easily available as alternatives to complete divestiture of financial and business holdings of concern.

Beyond the appointments process, there are problems with government personnel systems specific to the Foreign Service, the Civil Service, and to the military services. But for all three, there is one step we urge: *Expand the National Security Education Act of 1991 (NSEA) to include broad support for social sciences, humanities, and foreign languages in exchange for civilian government and military service.*

This expanded Act is the complement to the National Security Science and Technology Education Act (NSSTEA) and would provide college scholarship and loan forgiveness benefits for government service. Recipients could fulfill this service in a variety of ways: in the active duty military; in National Guard or Reserve units; in national security departments of the Civil Service; or in the Foreign Service. The expanded NSEA thus would provide an important means of recruiting high-quality people into military and civilian government service.

An effective and motivated Foreign Service is critical to the success of the Commission's restructuring proposal for the State Department, yet 25 percent fewer people are now taking the entrance exam compared to the mid-1980s. Those who do enter complain of poor management and inadequate professional education. *We therefore recommend that the Foreign Service system be improved by making leadership a core value of the State Department, revamping the examination process, and dramatically improving the level of on-going professional education.*

The Civil Service faces a range of problems from the aging of the federal workforce to institutional challenges in bringing new workers into government service to critical gaps in recruiting and retaining information technology professionals. To address these problems, the *Commission recommends eliminating recruitment hurdles, making the hiring process faster and easier, and designing professional education and retention programs worthy of full funding by Congress. Retaining talented information technology workers, too, will require greater incentives and the outsourcing of some IT support functions.*

The national security component of the Civil Service calls for professionals with breadth of experience in the interagency process and with depth of knowledge about policy issues. To develop these, *we recommend the establishment of a National Security Service Corps (NSSC) to* broaden the experience base of senior departmental managers and develop leaders who seek integrative solutions to national security policy problems. Participating departments would include Defense, State, Treasury, Commerce, Justice, Energy, and the new National Homeland Security Agency—the departments essential to interagency policy-making on key national security issues. While participating departments would retain control over their personnel, an interagency advisory group would design and monitor the rotational assignments and professional education that will be key to the Corps' success.

With respect to military personnel, reform is needed in the recruitment, promotion, compensation and retirement systems. Otherwise, the military will continue to lose its most talented personnel, and the armed services will be left with a cadre unable to handle the technological and managerial tasks necessary for a world-class 21st century force.

Beyond the significant expansion of scholarships and debt relief programs recommended in both the modified National Security Education Act and the newly created National Security Science and Technology Education Act, we recommend *substantial enhancements to the Montgomery GI Bill and strengthening recently passed and pending legislation that supports benefits—including transition, medical, and homeownership—for qualified veterans.* The GI Bill should be restored as a pure entitlement, be transferable to dependents if desired by career service members, and should equal, at the very least, the median tuition cost of four-year U.S. colleges. Payments should be accelerated to coincide with school term periods and be indexed to keep pace with college cost increases. In addition, Title 38 authority for veterans benefits should be modified to restore and substantially improve medical, dental, and VA home ownership benefits for all who qualify, but especially for career and retired service members. Taken as a package, such changes will help bring the best people into the armed service and persuade quality personnel to serve longer in order to secure greater rewards for their service.

While these enhancements are critical they will not, by themselves, resolve the quality recruitment and retention problems of the Services. *We therefore recommend significant modifications to military personnel legislation governing officer and enlisted career management, retirement, and compensation*—giving Service Secretaries more authority and flexibility to adapt their personnel systems and career management to meet 21st century requirements. This should include flexible compensation and retirement plans, exemption from "up-or-out" mandates, and reform of personnel systems to facilitate fluid movement of personnel. If we do not decentralize and modernize the governing personnel legislation, no military reform or transformation is possible. We also call for an Executive-Legislative working group to monitor, evaluate and share information about the testing and implementation of these recommendations. With bipartisan cooperation, our military will remain one of this nation's most treasured institutions and our safeguard in the changing world ahead.

The Role of Congress

While Congress has mandated many changes to a host of Executive Branch departments and agencies over the years, it has not fundamentally reviewed its own role in national security policy. Moreover, it has not reformed its own structure since 1949. At present, for example, every major defense program must be voted upon no fewer than eighteen times each year by an array of committees and subcommittees. This represents a very poor use of time for busy members of the Executive and Legislative Branches.

To address these deficiencies, *the Commission first recommends that the Congressional leadership conduct a thorough bicameral, bipartisan review of the Legislative Branch's relationship to national security and foreign policy.* The House Speaker, Majority, and Minority leaders and the Senate Majority and Minority leaders must work with the President and his top aides to bring proposed reforms to this Congress by the beginning of its second session.

From that basis, *Congressional and Executive Branch leaders must build programs to encourage members to acquire knowledge and experience in national security.* These programs should include ongoing education, greater opportunities for serious overseas travel, more legislature-to-legislature exchanges, and greater participation in wargames.

Greater fluency in national security matters must be matched by structural reforms. *A comprehensive review of the Congressional committee structure is needed* to ensure that it reflects the complexity of 21st century security challenges and of U.S. national security priorities. Specifically *we recommend merging appropriations subcommittees with their respective authorizing committees so that the new merged committees will authorize and appropriate within the same bill.* This should decrease the bureaucratic redundancy of the budget process and allow more time to be devoted to the oversight of national security policy.

An effective Congressional role in national security also requires ongoing Executive-Legislative consultation and coordination. The Executive Branch must ensure a sustained effort in consultation and devote resources to it. For its part, Congress must make consultation a higher priority, in part by *forming a permanent consultative group composed of the Congressional leadership and the Chairpersons and Ranking Members of the main committees involved in national security.* This will form the basis for sustained dialogue and greater support in times of crisis.

The Commission notes, in conclusion, that some of its recommendations will save money, while others call for more expenditure. We have not tried to "balance the books" among our recommendations, nor have we held financial implications foremost in mind during our work. We consider any money that may be saved a second-order benefit. We consider the provision of additional resources to national security, where necessary, to be investments, not costs, in *first-order* national priorities.

Finally, *we strongly urge the new President and the Congressional leadership to establish some mechanism to oversee the implementation of the recommendations proffered here.* Once some mechanism is chosen, the President must ensure that responsibility for implementing the recommendations of this Commission be given explicitly to senior personnel in both the Executive and Legislative Branches of government. The press of daily obligations is such that unless such delegation is made, and those given responsibility for implementation are held accountable for their tasks, the necessary reforms will not occur. The stakes are high. We of this Commission believe that many thousands of American lives, U.S. leadership among the community of nations, and the fate of U.S. national security itself are at risk unless the President and the Congress join together to implement the recommendations set forth in this report.

Appendix III
Global Democracy
Security Organization (NATO II): Charter (draft)[*]

The Parties to this Treaty reaffirm their faith in the purposes and principles of the Charter of the United Nations and their desire to live in peace with all peoples and all governments.

They are determined to safeguard the freedom, common heritage and civilisation of their peoples, founded on the principles of democracy, individual liberty and the rule of law. They seek to promote stability and well-being in that portion of the global commons that they share.

They are resolved to unite their efforts for collective defence and for the preservation of peace and security. They therefore agree to this Global Democracy Security Organization Charter:

Article 1
The Parties undertake, as set forth in the Charter of the United Nations, to settle any international dispute in which they may be involved by peaceful means in such a manner that international peace and security and justice are not endangered, and to refrain in their international relations from the threat or use of force in any manner inconsistent with the purposes of the United Nations.

[*] Based on the North Atlantic Treaty Organization charter, available at
http://www.nato.int/docu/basictxt/treaty.htm

Article 2

The Parties will contribute toward the further development of peaceful and friendly international relations by strengthening their free institutions, by bringing about a better understanding of the principles upon which these institutions are founded, and by promoting conditions of stability and well-being. They will seek to eliminate conflict in their international economic policies and will encourage economic collaboration between any or all of them.

Article 3

In order to more effectively achieve the objectives of this Treaty, the Parties, separately and jointly, by means of continuous and effective self-help and mutual aid, will maintain and develop their individual and collective capacity to resist armed attack.

Article 4

The Parties will consult together whenever, in the opinion of any of them, the territorial integrity, political independence or security of any of the Parties is threatened.

Article 5

The Parties agree that an armed attack against one or more of them shall be considered an attack against them all and consequently they agree that, if such an armed attack occurs, each of them, in exercise of the right of individual or collective self-defence recognised by Article 51 of the Charter of the United Nations, will assist the Party or Parties so attacked by taking forthwith, individually and in concert with the other Parties, such action as it deems necessary, including the use of armed force, to restore and maintain the security of their shared portion of the global commons defined by their collective borders.

Any such armed attack and all measures taken as

a result thereof shall immediately be reported to the Security Council. Such measures shall be terminated when the Security Council has taken the measures necessary to restore and maintain international peace and security.

Article 6

For the purpose of Article 5, an armed attack on one or more of the Parties is deemed to include an armed attack:

- on the territory of any of the Parties in their shared portions of the global commons;
- on the forces, vessels, or aircraft of any of the Parties, when in or over these territories.

Article 7

This Treaty does not affect, and shall not be interpreted as affecting in any way the rights and obligations under the Charter of the Parties which are members of the United Nations, or the primary responsibility of the Security Council for the maintenance of international peace and security.

Article 8

Each Party declares that none of the international engagements now in force between it and any other of the Parties or any third State is in conflict with the provisions of this Treaty and undertakes not to enter into any international engagement in conflict with this Treaty.

Article 9

The Parties hereby establish a Council, on which each of them shall be represented, to consider matters concerning the implementation of this Treaty. The Council shall be so organised as to be able to meet promptly at any time. The Council shall set up such subsidiary bodies as may be necessary; in particular it shall establish immediately a defence committee which shall recommend measures for the implementation of Articles 3 and 5.

Article 10
The Parties may, by unanimous agreement, invite any other democracy sharing its institutions, principles, and values and in a position to further the principles of this Treaty and to contribute to the security of the North Atlantic area to accede to this Treaty. Any State so invited may become a Party to the Treaty by depositing its instrument of accession with the Government of the United States of America. The Government of the United States of America will inform each of the Parties of the deposit of each such instrument of accession.

Article 11
This Treaty shall be ratified and its provisions carried out by the Parties in accordance with their respective constitutional processes. The instruments of ratification shall be deposited as soon as possible with the Government of the United States of America, which will notify all the other signatories of each deposit. The Treaty shall enter into force between the States which have ratified it as soon as the ratifications of the majority of the signatories have been deposited and shall come into effect with respect to other States on the date of the deposit of their ratifications.

Article 12
After the Treaty has been in force for ten years, or at any time thereafter, the Parties shall, if any of them so requests, consult together for the purpose of reviewing the Treaty, having regard for the factors then affecting peace and security in the North Atlantic area, including the development of universal as well as regional arrangements

under the Charter of the United Nations for the maintenance of international peace and security.

Article 13

After the Treaty has been in force for twenty years, any
Party may cease to be a Party one year after its notice
of denunciation has been given to the Government of
the United States of America, which will inform the
Governments of the other Parties of the deposit of each
notice of denunciation.

Article 14

This Treaty, of which the English and French texts are
equally authentic, shall be deposited in the archives of the
Government of the United States of America. Duly certi-
fied copies will be transmitted by that Government to the
Governments of other signatories.

About the Author

Gary Hart represented the state of Colorado in the U.S. Senate from 1975 to 1987. He is currently Wirth Chair Professor at the University of Colorado, Distinguished

Courtesy Denver Post

Fellow at the New America Foundation, and a member of the Council on Foreign Relations. He was co-chair of the U.S. Commission on National Security for the 21st Century. The Commission performed the most comprehensive review of national security since 1947, predicted the terrorist attacks on America, and proposed a sweeping overhaul of U.S. national security structures and policies for the post-Cold War new century and the age of terrorism. Senator Hart is the author of seventeen books, including *The Courage of Our Convictions: A Manifesto For Democrats*, *The Shield and the Cloak: Security in the Commons*, and *God and Caesar in America: An Essay on Religion and Politics in America* (Fulcrum).